THE COMMUNITY ACTIVIST'S HANDBOOK

THE
COMMUNITY
ACTIVIST'S
HANDBOOK

A Guide to Organizing,
Financing,
and Publicizing
Community Campaigns

By John Huenefeld

BEACON PRESS *Boston*

To my father, Arnold Huenefeld

Contents

Introduction

There are some 80,000 units of local government (counties and smaller) in these United States of America—run by over half a million elected officials and policed by 30,000 separate law enforcement agencies. They spend more than 45 billion dollars a year. Most of us live under the authority (and share the costs) of several of these units, since our 35,000 cities, towns, and townships are overlapped by a variety of regional agencies and by specialized, independent school and improvement districts.

These local governing agencies exert great influence on the way we live. They are the dominant level of government within our federal system in such matters as the exercise of police power, public education below the college level, recreation, regulation of land use, and such unglamorous yet essential services as waste disposal.

Furthermore, local government is the only echelon of our national system on which most of us can exert any direct influence, or with which we can feel any personal identity—except during moments of patriotic drama. The nation, the states, even most of the counties are sprawling conglomerates in which most individuals can function politically only as minute statistics—barely affecting the averages, trends, and probabilities on which governing decisions are based. Today many of our cities and their suburbs seem destined to be further depersonalized through absorption into multi-state supercities—Megalopolis—unless some measure of independence and distinctiveness and personal identity can be preserved through more creative and forceful community responses to our complex problems and opportunities. But we should note that political scientists and research agencies have been generally unanimous in contending that it is on this still somewhat personal local level that government functions most poorly. Few of the half-million officials in charge have professional qualifications for their jobs or receive enough income from them to make them more than incidental hobbies. The more imaginative and talented public servants drift upward in the federal system to operate on the more impersonal levels of regional, state, and national government.

The motives of the half-million who seek and win power on the local level are varied. Certainly some serve because of civic dedication to the community—and place in our service talents and experience worth many times the pittances we pay them for it, if we pay them anything. But the pursuit of special, personal interests, the exercise of pure ego, and aspirations for advancement to other levels of government and politics often place local governing agencies in control of people who bring little imagination, energy, knowledge, or experience to the tasks at hand.

Too often, when citizens complain about inertia and noncreativity in local government, the time servers in command reply: "If you don't like what's happening, why don't you run for office?" Certainly this is the most direct action you can take to change what you don't like about (or supply what is missing in) your community. Yet often the time demands are such that you cannot realistically pursue such a course. Whatever an irritated official object of your criticism may imply, this is certainly no reason to disqualify yourself from taking exception to "the way things are"—and doing something about it.

Unless we come to grips locally—in varied and personal ways—with the significant problems of our social existence, we will almost certainly evolve into a homogenous nation of nearly identical communities, reacting inflexibly and statistically to national trends without regard to local differences. To prevent such a dull society, we need a far-flung underground of community activists who dare to translate their personal aspirations—or their communities' peculiarities and potentialities—into political enterprise, with a forcefulness which will keep local government on its toes.

This handbook is written to encourage that underground.

But whether you are really driving for significant community innovations or simply presiding over the routine and noncontroversial functions of an existing organization or committee, it should provide some practical assistance for all who conduct meetings, seek publicity, raise money, or otherwise engage in part-time, voluntary civic activity.

To raise problems and demonstrate possibilities which are applicable to a wide range of circumstances and a wide variety of communities, the handbook offers examples which may be more complex than the situations you expect to encounter. Please do not assume from this that the book is not directed to your concerns or that it is not meant to deal with relatively simple situations. The author merely assumes that in the course of somewhat complex examples we will encounter more of the specific problems and possibilities with which you'll want to become familiar than we would by sticking to simpler demonstrations.

Hopefully, the book will be of some assistance in directly instructing people who will work with you in special capacities. The chapters on publicity and fund raising, for instance, might be offered as basic guidelines for the individuals who will head up those vital functions in your adventure. And the appendices should help when you delegate people to prepare the basic documents of organization and planning.

Perhaps the handbook will also help bring some awkward realities into the open where they can be freely discussed and dealt with by your core leadership group. The necessity for shuffling assignments to remove nonperformers from the chain of command or the subtle maneuvers by which a founding group maintains control while broadening its base through democratic participation processes are matters your steering committee might find easier to talk about once they've all established a common base by reading this not too extended volume.

Some of the techniques described in the following pages may strike the reader as cynically Machiavellian—the staging of pseudo-events to intrigue the press, the creation of semi-honorary advisory posts as a diplomatic means of removing nonperformers from the chain of command, the use of a steering committee as an invisible nominating committee, the calculated flattery of potential financial contributors through advice-seeking and superficial appointments, the use of people's guilt feelings as a basis for discipline.

But it would be hypocritical to ignore these techniques; they are commonly employed by the loftiest-minded community leaders now getting results in your society. You may shy from them if you wish, but at least you should recognize them as standard components of the leadership arsenal.

In recent years the Kennedys and others have created a mystique about systematic campaigning—an impression that there are powerful secrets known only to a few professionals which will achieve spectacular results. As you read this book, you will discover no such secrets—for the simple reason that they do not exist. The impression of miraculous techniques is created by the enormous amount of planning and preparation which such campaigners are willing to commit to an enterprise before they expose it to public inspection. You will be halfway through this book before you reach the conventional starting point of most amateur projects. Do not be discouraged by the time commitments this seems to imply. Every hour spent in such systematic preparation will be returned to you later twofold—in the prevention of wasteful milling about and inefficiency.

The book is designed to help you cope with the more complex types of volunteer activity. Certainly you'll take shortcuts, and eliminate entire components which do not seem necessary because of the nature of your specific project. But by covering all of the ground thoroughly, the handbook will help you avoid costly oversights.

More than anything, this book should provide a focus for what you already know about people, about organization, about purposeful dialogue with the public. Your reading should be viewed as an experience, not a search for a formula. Many of the examples will lead you to think: "I've been there before." The author's purpose is primarily to help you recognize and organize and use what you learned when you were there.

So—welcome to the underground. May it be said of you, when the time comes for epitaphs, "The world will never be the same again."

JOHN HUENEFELD

Bedford, Massachusetts
September 8, 1969

PART ONE

Planning

Having Fun Changing Things

Forming a Steering Committee

Finding the Facts You Need

How to Conduct a Meeting

Hostility Control

Creating the Right First Impression in Public

Timetables, Organization, Budgets, and By-Laws

CHAPTER ONE

Having fun changing things

So you think that vacant lot down by the water reservoir would make a great recreation area. Or you're convinced that a sympathetic counselor in the police department could keep a lot of youngsters from graduating from pranks to crime. Or you believe it's time people who really wanted to build some low-cost housing units took control of your local housing authority.

Whether you're running for mayor or merely trying to get the garbage picked up on time, whether you're an established leader in a small village or a brash upstart in a city, you'll find that certain fundamental techniques can help you expand your own concerns and talents into an organized campaign capable of achieving real community changes.

But who are you?

The mere fact that you are reading this book suggests that you are at least potentially a leader of such change, because you recognize the possibilities of direct citizen action. You may have a specific project in mind or you may simply feel that your community is too uncreative and needs to be enlivened by a spirited campaign. You may be a leader of an already established group, or you may be an "army of one." In any case, you have identified yourself as a potential leader in seeking community changes.

Creating social change on the community level often seems more difficult than it is because people view it as a spontaneous process. A group of citizens get together, commit themselves to a cause, and then hold meeting after meeting in the hope that by devoting enough time to sharing their commitment, they will discover a path to achievement.

Most such meetings are monumental wastes of time. Mass meetings are seldom effective agents of social action unless an organized leadership has done its homework—has developed information on which such a meeting can make intelligent decisions, and a plan which will put those at the meeting to work in a productive manner. Nothing weakens a project as much as large meetings which reach only very generalized decisions and from which no specific follow-up action results.

Actually, three or four people who can work well together and who are prepared to follow a few systematic guidelines are far more effective than a hall full of undirected and uncoordinated human energy. The techniques of organization and persuasion which this small group must employ are neither mysterious nor difficult. But they do require patience, planning, and coordination—qualities less likely to be found in a large and spontaneous gathering than in a small group dedicated to setting the stage properly before it subjects its project to public view.

The reason most projects of this sort start in public meetings—and either fade into group apathy or struggle in disorganized fashion toward disappointing results—is lack of leadership. Yet on the community level, leadership itself is not a rare quality confined to an elite few. Your recognition of the possibility of change makes you a potential leader. Your willingness to call together three or four likely people to start pursuing that change deliberately and logically will make you a leader in fact.

Your leadership will be confirmed by the progress of the project. If progress is apparent, others will become more and more committed to following your guidance. And you will grow in self-confidence, and become firmer and more forceful and more productive as a leader.

So we get back to that question: who are you? You are —if you're willing to put yourself forward as such—a potential community leader who can look forward not only to helping create a better community, but also to satisfying personal growth as your leadership is confirmed and broadened by the responsiveness of a group of your fellow citizens.

Community leaders—both the official, elected variety and the informal, citizen-action variety—are limited in their accomplishments by the amount of active public support they can marshal. When things do not progress satisfactorily, they are prone to blame "public apathy." Much of this apathy stems from the widespread attitude that civic projects are dull and unrewarding work—unwarranted claims on an individual's free time. But, in fact, taking part in a well-planned, well-led civic project can be far more entertaining, educational, and personally satisfying than most parties or television programs or other objects of your neighbors' leisure time. You'll find it much easier to win recruits for your cause if you present the undertaking with such a positive attitude.

Recall how often, when someone asks you to help in a volunteer project, a touch of demagoguery comes into play. The recruiter seeks to arouse your indignation about a problem or a strong appeal is made to your sense of duty. This approach implies that there is nothing in it for you except an opportunity to serve others, and you can probably identify enough instances in which you are already serving (other organizations, your church or synagogue, your family) to provide a good alibi if you're at all disposed to decline.

Even if you accept such an appeal to duty, it's natural to do so with a touch of self-righteousness. Later, when the novelty wears off and the going gets a bit rougher, this self-righteousness reminds you that you really owe nothing to the project, so no one can complain if you accomplish nothing.

It must be admitted that grim fanaticism has sometimes accomplished miracles. But let's face it, even if you are fanatic about your project, only a few people will respond with equal fervor; and fanaticism burns out all but the most dedicated in a hurry.

So, as you set out to overcome public apathy by recruiting co-workers for your project, at least consider another approach. Think a bit more deeply about your own motives. Whatever grand rationalizations we construct for ourselves, most of us really get involved in civic projects for very personal reasons. We're bored; we realize that most of the excitement of life comes from other people—and here's a chance to get exposed to that excitement. We're lonely—and we realize that people often communicate more honestly and fundamentally with each other when they're working together than when they're playing together. We're unsure of ourselves—and we've read enough to realize that few of us really find out who we are until we feel the responses of other people to our personalities and intellects.

In short, civic activity is less expensive than gin, more exciting than most old movie re-runs on television, and a very satisfying arena for the growth of personality and intellect. Why an activity with such possibilities should be urged upon others as grim duty is one of the mysteries of the contemporary civic mentality.

Examine your own aspirations until you can identify enough personal value in the project to make it worthwhile, whether it succeeds in its stated objective or not. Then project that attitude as you set out to recruit others to your cause.

If you are willing to take the initiative in getting a few susceptible people together, and if you will face your project with a (not too grim, please) determination to let it be fun for you and for others, it is possible to bring about very gratifying changes in the style of life of your community and to have a very satisfying personal experience while doing it.

But before you start recruiting others, do a little basic spadework. Invest a few hours in preliminary information gathering and tactical thinking. And out of this, develop a very concrete statement of what you want to accomplish.

Vague, over-generalized objectives are seldom met. The trick is to conceive of some specific development which will inevitably propel your community in the direction you want it to go.

Suppose, for example, that you're concerned about reports of teen-age drug addiction. With very little supporting evidence, you can easily inflame other indignant or worried parents into holding a public meeting and forming an organization "to combat the use of drugs by young people within the community." It may have some impact by alarming adults, who will then watch their children more closely, or by stirring the local police department and school officials to (probably temporary) heightened vigilance, but the results will be limited and short term because no specific and lasting improvement has been made in the conditions which caused the problem. On the other hand, if you're convinced that youngsters in your community get involved with drugs because they are bored and "looking for kicks," establishing a social and recreational center to relieve that boredom could be an effective contribution. Or if you conclude that the problem is caused by a conscious rejection of your adult society, a well-planned confrontation program of adult-youth panel discussions—on a broad scale—could convince many teen-agers that they can be more constructive in their rejection (and perhaps even persuade them that you don't warrant such extreme rejection). If you believe the root of the addiction is innocent experimentation, an informational program may be in order. Setting up a project to pursue any of these specific objectives will almost inevitably have a greater impact on the community climate of teen-age life than vague generalizations about "combating the use of drugs."

It is important that you examine such specific possibilities for dealing with general problems before you start organizing the project with others. People apply themselves to an enterprise most effectively when they are shown real possibilities—when they are convinced that meaningful progress is plausible. Even the small group with which you will develop detailed plans (to say nothing of the larger public which must eventually become involved) will drift away from the project if the project itself seems to be drifting.

Volunteer, amateur projects often fall apart while people are mentally milling around waiting for a group decision. Your first resolution should be: *never* leave it to a group to decide between spontaneous suggestions presented to it without forethought. While you should not insist every time that your proposals be adopted, you should *have a proposal ready* for each crucial point of decision, whether you're involved with a small preparatory group or with the larger public meetings that will eventually follow.

That is the essence of leadership.

To be prepared for even the first informal meeting, you'll need reliable background information. Don't launch into an exhaustive, singlehanded research program; save as much of the work as possible to be shared with others as the organization unfolds. But a few quiet conversations with public officials or interested professionals (clergymen, any social workers you know, friends who are lawyers or doctors or construction engineers) can give you a realistic outline of the possibilities for coping with a generalized problem or seizing a broad opportunity.

When you initiate these conversations, limit yourself to asking questions rather than making statements. Indicate your concern with the general subject area and *ask* for their suggestions about what might be done. When they mention specific possibilities, ask about the legal steps involved and the probable costs. But don't—particularly with public officials, who may not welcome private intrusion into their domains and who might begin planning defensive obstacles—declare your intention of doing anything specific. Save that until you know what can be done, have developed your own organizational "muscle," and are ready to move faster than official opponents.

And be careful not to use this exploratory information-gathering as a way to procrastinate by carrying it any further than necessary. You might ask about sources of dependable literature or specialized agencies and associations which could be of help, and you might take a quick look at the public library's card index, but leave the comprehensive research for later team effort. You're going to need it as a mechanism for getting other people involved.

When you have a general idea of what can be done, you must next consider a basic strategy for achieving it. Almost any campaign for community change will take one of three basic forms. The nature of the change you seek will, in many cases, dictate which approach you'll follow; where there is a choice, you may wish to delay it until others can help make it. But you'll want to start sorting the alternatives in your own mind at an early stage.

The simplest of these three basic approaches is to organize a private association of citizens who will undertake the project without official blessings or appropriations. This means your group will raise the necessary money, obtain the necessary volunteers, and proceed whether or not it has the approval of the community. What can be accomplished with such an approach is already well demonstrated in the community; most of its churches and synagogues are established on this basis.

Most communities have provisions for private use of certain public facilities (such as school buildings after school hours) for worthy purposes; religious and social service organizations may also offer facilities at very nominal costs. A dozen or so committed citizens can, therefore, sponsor and man a public information project at very little cost without winning official support. Fifty families banding together could support the part-time services of a professional to deal with mental health or educational problems or provide opportunities not available in the public health and educational systems. It is not uncommon for several families to cooperate in financing a vacation home or camp; why can't a hundred families just as easily finance a community recreation center?

The advantages of this approach are that it avoids the necessity for winning official public sanction, that it can go forward as rapidly as it wins the necessary recruits (without worrying about overcoming the opponents), that it is not subject to the often cumbersome limitations on the use of public money, and that it can stick to a limited objective without having to prove its value to the entire community. The disadvantages are that it revolves around a limited group and thus does not involve the community in the therapeutic exercise of coming openly and officially to grips with the problem at hand, and that it may cost more money than a limited group can raise through voluntary contributions or assessments.

The second basic approach is to organize an educational campaign which will create sufficiently strong public opinion to pressure an existing local official or agency into sponsoring and administering the change you wish to bring about. This approach will obviously cost its supporters less than a private association because they need only finance the public opinion campaign; if they succeed, further financing will come from the public treasury.

Perhaps the easiest way to give sharp focus to such a public opinion campaign is to circulate a petition. The simple task of soliciting signatures produces appropriate occasions for you and your colleagues to offer education and argument to the community. The existence of those signatures is concrete evidence of your success.

But the public opinion approach has one large disadvantage. Expressions of public opinion are seldom binding. Administration of the new program is often left in the hands of an official who may not be strongly committed to its success—or may, in fact, actually resent having been forced to undertake the venture. This is hardly calculated to insure persistent and energetic follow-up.

The third basic approach is to identify an elective public office or board which has the authority and the resources to carry out the innovation you wish to see made in the community, and seek election to that office—or organize a slate of candidates to seize control of a board. This is certainly the most direct approach —and probably the most exciting. It simplifies organization and recruiting because it has a clear-cut objective (victory on election day) which is easy to communicate. It eliminates problems in group decision-making because workers in a political campaign clearly expect the candidate or candidates to make most of the substantive decisions, whereas members of a cooperative venture expect to participate in all important decisions.

The major disadvantage of the political campaign is that it requires a different sort of commitment from you; a candidate cannot delegate as extensively as the chairman or president of a cooperative organization. The public will expect you, as a candidate, to speak for yourself. Your organized supporters can perform many tasks for you, but public representations of your cause will always require your presence. Furthermore, in the campaign—and after election—you cannot limit yourself to the specific innovative program you are promoting; you will be required to deal with other aspects of the elective position which may not particularly interest you. And you must operate on a tight, fast-moving time schedule. Everything must be done before election day. There is no such thing as being a week late and succeeding.

Once you've identified a specific innovation which can bring about the general type of change you hope to cause in the community, and determined from discreet preliminary investigation how you might go about achieving it, and committed yourself to provide initial leadership to get things started and keep them moving—you're ready to begin recruiting others to your cause and sharing the work and the fun. At first, all you'll need is three or four friends. Let's consider next how best to use them.

CHAPTER TWO

Forming a steering committee

Getting other people to work actively for a cause is perhaps the best way to win broad public support. When an individual becomes involved, his recruitment of other supporters is by no means limited to his agreed organizational assignments. His friends, his neighbors, his relatives, his professional associates will hear a great deal about the merits of your project—and such personal communication will yield more effective results on election day, or when you circulate petitions to influence a public agency, or when you begin general solicitation for contributions and manpower for a cooperative venture, than any number of handbills or form letters or newspaper ads.

The place to begin spreading your base of support is in establishing a leadership nucleus. This small leadership group will almost certainly dominate the later stages of the project. By picking the right people—and leading them through the right series of preliminary steps—you can multiply the chances for eventual success of your venture.

At the same time, organizing such a core group will enable you to share with others the work of getting the project underway. Remember that you, too, are supposed to be having fun, and the quickest way to spoil your fun is to load yourself down with too much work.

As soon as you've completed a cursory, personal examination of the possibilities, then, you should recruit a steering committee to help you plan and organize your project, enabling you to divide the preliminary work and establish the direction of the project before exposing it to possible opposition through public meetings and wide-scale recruiting. It will bring to your basic planning a variety of insights which can broaden and double-check your own conclusions and information.

Perhaps even more importantly, the work of the pre-

11

liminary steering committee will provide a means of testing the dedication, energy, competence, and dependability of people you will later have to depend upon for the performance of crucial assignments—when you're too close to the climax to have your timetable upset by nonperformers.

Don't worry about the representative nature of the steering committee; it should not be an exercise in parliamentary democracy. Democracy and diversity will be served later, when this committee presents its plans and proposals to a general membership meeting for endorsement or amendment and goes out of business—to be replaced by elected officers. The steering committee itself should be a closely knit group which works well together, sharing enough common information and insight that most of its decisions will be by general consensus rather than the formal counting of votes.

This suggests drawing heavily on your friends or on people with whom you've previously worked in other organizations —people who've already seen each other make mistakes, survive embarrassments, and preserve mutual respect despite the appalling discovery that you are all only human. Such a group can get down to cases fast without ego-protective shadowboxing.

But you should give a little thought to both the intellectual diversity and the public image of the small group you are going to assemble. If they're all from one church or club or other subsegment of the community, others may suspect the group of being a front for a limited special interest and be reluctant to join you when you start your general recruiting. If they're all from one specialized professional or educational background, their contributions of knowledge and experience will cover a narrower range than if they have differing backgrounds. Some diversity, then, is in order—as long as it does not present personality problems and gaps in understanding which will keep the group from communicating freely and intensely and working well together.

Three or four people will be enough; twice this number will be too many for well-knit, discreet preliminary planning. But unless you are sure of your people, it may be well to invite half a dozen to your first discussion; people do not view invitations to work sessions as mandatory social obligations, and you don't want to be bogged down if too few show up to get the project underway.

When you invite participation in the initial discussion, provide a general description of your objectives which will allow the disinterested to bow out gracefully. There should be as few superfluous people as possible at any of these crucial work sessions.

Don't arouse resentment by setting yourself up as an earth mover; people prefer to reach their own conclusions on that score. Instead of *"I've* called a meeting to see what we can do about the teen-age drug problem," try "Several people are meeting at my house to discuss what might be done about the teen-age drug problem." You don't have to claim sponsorship of an idea to insure your acceptance as a leader; that will follow naturally if you do a reasonable job of issuing the invitations, serving as host, opening the discussion, and displaying the background knowledge and ideas you have acquired.

If you anticipate that the work of this steering committee will be brief and simple, formal organization may be unnecessary —or even appear presumptuous. To get things started, you might prepare several copies of a brief outline of what you have learned and what you think could be done. Start the outline circulating among the early arrivers so that attention can be turned immediately to the business you want to discuss—instead of drifting through an awkward prelude of small-talk which leaves everyone wondering how to get started. Latecomers can monitor the conversation while they catch up by scanning the outline; declining to wait for that final arrival may reduce the time span of your meeting by twenty minutes and avoid a too-long meeting—the death of many a worthy project.

Start the discussion yourself by proposing bluntly that those who have assembled work together to organize a project along the lines of your outline. Guide the conversation with "What do you think?" questions, until someone else leads it in a positive new direction. Demonstrate your leadership by drawing the group back to meaningful subjects whenever it digresses.

In brief, proceed (diplomatically) as though you were the chairman of a formal meeting, even though the formalities have not been established. Volunteer to undertake certain obvious tasks yourself, but pull the others into the enterprise by asking frequently: "Now who's willing to do this?"

The specific objectives of this initial meeting should be the designation of a chairman, and the assignment of preliminary tasks to each person willing to participate. Additional officers are unnecessary in a group this small; designation of the convention slate of "vice chairman, secretary, treasurer" may, in fact, result in meaningless makework, as people attempt to act out their personal concepts of what such titles imply, rather than devoting themselves to the flexible tasks of preliminary planning and organization and recruiting.

By now we can assume that you are sufficiently committed to your project and concerned about its success to be willing to insure that it lives up to your aspirations by serving as its principal leader. This means you should be the chairman your steering committee selects as its only necessary act of formal organization.

Your initiative in arranging the meeting, plus the headstart your advance investigation has given you, will make it natural for the group to designate you as their chairman. But don't undermine your future prerogative of insisting that others share the leadership chores by nominating yourself.

Bring things gently and diplomatically to a point of decision by having prepared a "shadow" agenda in the form of a series of obvious statements which you intend to make at appropriate stages of the informal discussion. They might go something like this:

(1) "I gather from earlier conversations (while extending the invitations) that all of us are interested in doing something about the teen-age drug problem."

(2) "I asked the police chief and the high school principal what they thought about the problem; shall I review what they said?"

(3) "It seems obvious that to do something effective, we're going to have to set up an organization large enough to influence public opinion (or win an election, or finance a cooperative venture)."

(4) "To get things started, why don't we set ourselves up as a temporary steering committee to plan a general program, accumulate basic information, and prepare for a general organizational meeting?"

(5) "To make sure we aren't overlooking things, or getting our signals crossed, maybe someone should serve as chairman of this temporary steering committee until we set up a permanent organization."

By this point, you're almost certain to have the chairmanship urged on you by the rest of the group. But if someone else volunteers, be prepared to counter quickly with your own statement (something like: "Or, if you'd rather, since I've already done some spadework, I'll take it on until we have a general organizational meeting and an election"). Otherwise, simple good manners may cause the group to send your aspirations down the drain by putting them in charge of someone who hasn't had time to evaluate what is involved.

Once you're over this hurdle of constituting yourselves as a group with a purpose and a leader, things can proceed rapidly. But your first task as a leader may be to restrain the steering committee. Point out the necessity for being discreet—for not tipping your hand to potential opponents until you're ready, by such individual actions as "letters to the editor."

And point out to the group the advantage of finding other people to do as much of the work as possible as a means of broadening your base of support and stimulating participation in the eventual, public organizational meeting. A particularly good way is by recruiting others to perform essential research—collecting information and ideas for the edification of the public and the guidance of the general organizational meeting.

The first task of the steering committee, then, might be to list questions which should be answered through such research before a final program is adopted. As chairman, you should then delegate one member of the steering committee to supervise, coordinate, and monitor this information-gathering process. But ask all members of the steering committee to assist in recruiting members of this information-gathering team. This will insure that your first opportunity to spread your base of support will reach across a broader cross section of the community than if one individual recruited all the researchers.

The person assigned to supervise this task may wish to visit each researcher to outline the work to be done or call all the recruits together for a specialized meeting. In either case, determine immediately how the individual in charge plans to proceed, as a means of reenforcing his or her commitment to proceed promptly.

You can demonstrate the feasibility of rapid progress (and your dynamic leadership) by proposing that the recruitment of these researchers be undertaken immediately—at that first meeting of the steering committee—by a quick telephone campaign. Ask each person to think of the most likely recruit they know. Then gather around the telephone and take turns calling your own nominees, making such a simple statement as, "We've set up a steering committee to look into the possibility of doing something about the teen-age drug problem and we wonder if you'd help us out by getting together some background information from one of the sources we can identify."

We won't dwell here on the details (that's the business of Chapter Three). The point is simply that this is an opportunity to strike while the iron is hot (and your steering committee is fresh) to begin broadening your base of support and demonstrating that quick progress is possible.

And the exercise will serve another vital purpose. It takes a while for people to become comfortable in their roles as leaders of a new venture. Procrastination only breeds more of the same. The best way to make sure that your steering committee will start moving is to start it yourself—right there in front of each other—with such an exercise as turnabout telephone recruiting, which enables everybody to get over his initial awkwardness and profit by one another's examples.

Now that you've got things in motion, you should agree upon the specific tasks which the steering committee must accomplish to convert the enterprise into a broadbased public organization. Two of these tasks are so fundamental that they should be undertaken through discussion by the committee as a whole; the others may be delegated to specific individuals—or perhaps teams of two individuals—though a review by the entire committee will be in order before any general organizational meeting is attempted.

The two basic tasks are (1) choosing the specific objective which will most effectively lead to the sort of change you want to make in your community, and (2) choosing the general approach you will follow in achieving that specific objective.

For example:

Your discussion of the teen-age drug problem leads to a number of suggestions. You could work for tougher police action, or for better communication between generations, or for more public information, or even for repeal of drug laws. Whichever you choose as your specific objective becomes in itself a means of bringing about a changed set of conditions in your community regarding the general problem of teen-agers and drugs.

If there are really several more or less equally feasible specific means of achieving your general goal, the steering committee and its recruited information gatherers may wish to prepare and investigate several alternative proposals for the eventual public organizational meeting. But this presents the danger that your organization may be so attracted to several possibilities that it dilutes its energy by attempting too much; generally speaking, it is best that the steering committee thrash out the alternatives and agree upon a specific proposal on which a general membership can take action without undue delay and repetitious deliberation.

As Chapter One pointed out, there are three alternative approaches to achieving almost any specific community innovation. Let's say your objective is to help relieve slum conditions by creating more—and better—low-cost housing. You could approach it as a cooperative, semi-private venture, as a public opinion campaign, or as an election campaign.

As a cooperative, you would perhaps seek to persuade other individuals and foundations and even investment institutions to pool their money and set an example as enlightened de-

velopers and landlords—actually building and renting or selling appropriate housing units, and continuing to reinvest the proceeds in expanding the project.

By marshaling public opinion, you might present the public housing authority or the city council with a petition signed by a major portion of the community, demonstrating that the people of the community are behind aggressive official action to produce more low-cost housing.

As a candidate, or slate of candidates, you might attempt to win an effective voice on, or outright control of, your community's housing board or municipal council in the next local election, with the avowed intention of using your political authority to sponsor development of public, low-cost housing.

Choosing the most effective specific objective and the most feasible approach will require some assessment of the character of the community and its political structure. The official calendar will play a part; there may not be an election scheduled within the time period you've established for getting results. Your municipal charter (or the legislative regulations which serve as implied "charters" for many communities) may have limited the possibilities for official action; you may have to decide whether to broaden your goals to include amending the charter before taking further action.

Consequently, though consideration of detailed plans should begin early in the career of the steering committee, you may want to delay final decisions until your researchers have fully outlined the possibilities. But keep in mind the wisdom of making the basic strategy decisions and tactical plans within the intimate confines of the steering committee (for later consideration by the general organization), rather than expecting a larger group to tunnel its way through the many factors involved under the hurried circumstances of a public meeting.

While the steering committee as a whole continues to meet and shape overall plans, there are some specific tasks which you, as chairman, should delegate to individual members. One member must coordinate the research effort (see Chapter Three). Another should coordinate preliminary publicity to attract attention to your eventual organizational meeting (see Chapter Six). As your plan unfolds, others should prepare schedules, organization charts, budgets, and by-laws (see Chapter Seven).

It may seem easier to depend on a few stalwart enthusiasts to do a lot of work than to recruit scores of people to do small assignments. But therein lies a key to successful campaigning which you can't afford to overlook—and to which we will refer time and time again throughout this handbook.

The best way to win broad public support for any community improvement venture—be it a cooperative, the development of public opinion, or a political campaign—is to recruit as many people as possible to work on the project. Each recruit, in addition to his assigned tasks, will inevitably mount a small personal campaign of his own in his normal contacts with the people he knows and sees regularly. So the more jobs your steering committee can manufacture during the planning phase, the better off you are. Recruiting is the most intensive (and dependable) form of campaigning.

That is the essence of the new style of participatory politics. It gets people excited; it works; and furthermore, it reduces the demand for the hardest to come by commodity of any campaign—money—because it achieves by voluntary manpower much that you'd otherwise have to buy with cash.

The establishment of a steering committee—and the subsequent planning and recruiting—is on a somewhat different footing if you have already decided in advance to be a candidate for public office as a means of achieving your general goal. You must still make your appeal on the basis of a worthwhile objective to which others will be willing to commit their time and talent and money. But you have eliminated all the questions of leadership—you're clearly the leader, without the necessity for group endorsement. You have diminished the requirement for democratic niceties; supporters will generally accord the candidate the clear prerogative of making the important decisions.

Otherwise, however, little has changed. The techniques of planning and organizing, of recruiting, of stirring enthusiasm through personal involvement, of gathering essential background information, are the same whether you are a candidate, a petition writer, or the founder of a cooperative.

If you are thinking in terms of a political campaign, don't be bashful about asking other people to help. Give them something respectable (in addition to you as a person) to work for by stating what you hope to accomplish after your election, and unless they disapprove of you as an individual, most people will enlist and serve with at least the same fervor they'd bring to a less personal venture. In fact, because of the unambiguity of leadership (the certainty that it will be you, and not them, who faces most of the heat)—and because of the drama and excitement of politics—you may find them even more eager to join in an election campaign than in another type of project.

As noted before, it is important that the steering committee make basic decisions *before* you attempt to organize publicly. Large meetings of casually interested people will not be able to explore the possibilities and the problems in sufficient depth. Such meetings tend to solve their frustrations by lunging for the first plausible course of action, rather than searching for the most effective course.

Before it attempts public organization, then, the steering committee should have attempted to anticipate the entire career of the project and to outline a plan of action for each stage of that career. While subsequent general meetings—and experience—may modify those plans, only the existence of such a "road map" can prevent the deadliest disease of extracurricular volunteer organizations: the collapse of interest and commitment because of lack of direction and obvious progress.

First, your steering committee should make a firm choice of the specific objective through which it hopes to achieve its general goal. Unless the objective you choose clearly dictates one of the three basic approaches to community change outlined earlier—a cooperative venture, a public opinion campaign, or an election candidacy—your next decision is: Which of these approaches is most feasible for obtaining the specific objective the committee has adopted?

Before we go into some of the considerations which

should influence these basic decisions—and before you throw up your hands and ask: "How can a bunch of amateurs make such decisions?"—let's examine a basic technique. We might call it "what-if" brainstorming.

Brainstorming is a creative technique popularized a decade or more ago by management and promotion specialists to make sure that a wide range of possibilities was considered before a decision was reached. The rules are quite simple. Someone states the question at hand. Then, with the understanding that nobody is to criticize or ridicule anything said, all members of the group begin stating (with a minimum of elaboration) every possible solution that comes to mind—no matter how farfetched. One member of the group lists every suggestion for later consideration—but the suggestions are made orally so that everybody hears everything; this way, one person's idea may stimulate a related but better idea from another. (The ad men call this feature "hitchhiking.") No attempt to evaluate the suggestions or make decisions is allowed during the brainstorming session. After it's over, whoever is to make the decision takes the list of suggestions, weeds and combines, and shapes from them an answer to the problem.

In your steering committee, you can use a variation of this technique to sort out the possibilities as you choose your specific objective and your basic approach. Start by stating the general goal you've agreed to pursue. Then ask everyone present to suggest any specific, feasible community innovations which would lead to that goal. After you've listed the possibilities, go through them one by one, asking "What if?" in each instance. For example:

Your general goal is to provide your community with public bus service—thus saving hundreds of families the expense of a second car by getting Papa to the train station or the downtown office or Mama to the supermarket. One member takes notes while the steering committee starts suggesting every way of accomplishing this objective which comes to mind.

"Let's promote a bond issue to establish a public bus line."

"Why not try to persuade some private company to give us bus service on a profitable basis?"

"To do that, what we really need is a survey to show how many people would use the service."

"Instead of a survey, why not collect orders for monthly tickets, or something like that, to show either the town fathers or a private company how much money could be taken in from the very beginning?"

"If we're going to do that, it might be just as easy to get people to pledge a small investment to organize their own bus line. A lot of families should be willing to come up with a hundred dollars or more to escape the expense of a second car."

"Why don't we just create enough public demand to force the town government into figuring out how to do it and getting it done?"

After this process has run its course—and the flow of new suggestions seems to be ending—you as chairman simply take the list of suggestions and start back through it to collect ideas for methods of achieving the alternative objectives which are now before the group. You do this by asking "What if?" in relation to each earlier suggestion.

"All right, what if we decided to promote a bond issue to finance the establishment of a public bus service. How would we go about it?"

"Let's file a petition to get it on the ballot for next year's election."

"You'd need a real plan to get the votes. What we should do is file a petition requiring the City Council to appoint a study committee to prepare the bond proposal."

"I don't think a petition could force them to do it. But we could collect so many voters' signatures that they'd be afraid to ignore it."

"Wouldn't it be just as easy to elect some of our own people to the City Council to push the idea from the inside?"

A similar "What if?" discussion of each feasible course of action on the list will focus the possibilities in everyone's mind.

Then you might begin reducing the list to more manageable proportions by eliminating from further discussion all courses of action except those which a quick poll of the group shows have gained some support.

The surviving proposals should again be subjected to the "What if?" approach in terms of the three basic approaches to community action:

"Now what would happen if we tried to tackle this one as a cooperative venture—raising money from subscriptions or pledges instead of depending on public financing?"

". . . What if we depended entirely on public opinion? How would we accomplish this specific result that way?"

". . . What if we put up a candidate committed to this objective? What office should we try to win and how do we do it?"

You can't expect to cover all the necessary ground in one evening, especially at that first meeting of your steering group when their thoughts on the project are relatively uninformed. In fact, you'll want to play this "What if?" game several times, repetitively, to keep everyone's thoughts (and the new information you're receiving from your researchers) in sharp focus. But each time you do it, you'll find the process getting shorter as certain considerations become more obvious and a consensus begins to develop. In two, three, or four such sessions it is almost inevitable that a feasible plan of action will have taken shape.

There are, of course, other ways of deciding on a basic course of action. You might simply ask each steering committee member, at the first meeting, to agree to come back to the second meeting with his own proposal. Hear each other out, combine good ideas, and adopt the plan which gains the most support. Or collect outline suggestions from sympathetic professionals. Or, if you have money to spend, enlist a consultant to prepare one or more proposals.

Whichever course you pursue, you should make certain that at appropriate points in the consideration of any plan, reference is made to the nature of the community and the nature of probable public reactions.

What considerations are determined by whether your

community is urban, suburban, small town, or rural? Is the range of personal incomes so great that interest would be limited to one segment—and opposition predictable from another? Does the project itself have controversial overtones which would offend the "conventional wisdom" of the citizenry? (Remember, to some people *any* public service is socialistic, and that's freely translated as communistic. Is yours that kind of community—and if so, how are you going to make your proposal respectable?)

The smaller the community, the greater the opportunity for person-to-person campaigning—by far the most effective kind. But a large community will be less subject to irrational vetoes by one bloc or one very powerful community leader. The existence of local news media has an enormous bearing on your planning. In an urban community the scope of concerns of metropolitan media may dictate a very spectacular plan to achieve journalistic attention and thus publicity.

In a city you may want to lean toward tactics which allow lunch-hour meetings and campaigning. In suburbia you'll have to stick to evenings and week-ends if you want male participation; but if it's a project for housewives, the excuse for mid-morning coffee klatches could be a powerful recruiting and campaigning aid.

It is, of course, possible that you are planning a project for a nongeographic community—a proposal for your professional association, or some regional special interest group, or an alumni organization. Or you could be concerned with a specialized institutional community—a school, a convalescent home, a prison, a labor union. Review the special characteristics of any such community—and their impact on your choice of plans—just as though they were geographic communities.

If it seems to you that such a thorough examination of the possibilities is unnecessary—you're the boss. (Certainly if your original object is your own political candidacy for a specific office, you've already eliminated many of the alternatives.)

But before you turn away too readily, recall the efforts of those prisoners in *The Bridge on the River Kwai*. When their captors prodded them to start showing immediate results, they began quickly completing a few yards of the bridge each day—

but the whole structure soon collapsed in midstream. When their captors then agreed to let the prisoners do it their own way, they seemingly wasted days planning and plotting and preparing—yet the moment they began construction they made up the lost time in a hurry, with a sound structure that amazed their guards. Playing the "What if?" game repetitively for, say, three or four evenings while your research team is doing its work—and the preliminary publicity and attendance-promotion plans for your organizational meeting are being worked out by individual co-ordinators—should be a pleasant and not too taxing way to insure your project against a midstream collapse.

CHAPTER THREE

Finding the facts you need

While your steering committee is thrashing out the campaign plan and setting the stage for later public activities, the research segment of your organization should already be growing (and developing its recruiting skills) in private. For before you expose your proposal to possible opposition, you will need to arm yourself with background information regarding its costs, benefits, reliability, etc.

When members of your steering committee recruit people they know to start gathering this information, these initial workers may be motivated by nothing more than curiosity or friendship. But once they get involved—once they become your "experts" in particular aspects of the project—they will inevitably become increasingly partisan and dedicated. This very process of involving others is the real beginning of your campaign; once you've recruited your first workers, you've started gathering the snowball which can eventually achieve your goal.

After preparing a list of questions whose answers would prove helpful to the project, your steering committee should be able to enlist three or four times its number in brief, interesting research projects. To make the jobs you're offering palatable—to make it obvious that they can be done in a reasonable amount of time—you should parcel out research assignments on the basis of sources to be covered, rather than questions to be answered. Give the complete set of questions to every researcher you recruit and assign each to collect information and ideas regarding any of the questions from a single source.

The sources you'll want to cover (and, of course, the questions you'll want to ask) will depend on the nature of your project. However, the general guidelines offered here should lead fairly alert researchers to most of the possibilities.

26

Five broad source areas will provide a wealth of background information about techniques, costs, legal requirements, available external assistance, and relevant experience in other communities.

First, your researchers will want to examine specialized publications—books and periodicals—devoted to the general subject area. Secondly, they should interview all public officials or agencies—local, state, and federal—directly concerned with the type of problem or service your project is centered around (remembering, as they do, the previous admonition against premature hand-tipping). Next, they should seek relevant information or guidelines from professional and similarly specialized private associations concerned with the subject area or from individual professionals within the community whose civic spirit makes them willing to talk without fees. Furthermore, when and if it is plausible that the products or services of business enterprises might be employed in the project you envision, such companies should be invited to submit whatever material they consider appropriate. And finally, an effort should be made to identify other communities which have tried similar projects, in order to obtain some insight into their experiences.

You can expand the reach of your research considerably by appending some final questions to each interview with any of the above sources: "Who else do you recommend we talk with? What publications should we read? Do you know anyone who could tell us about experiences with similar problems or projects in other communities?"

Divide the research into limited segments. Send one person to the library to scan the material readily available there; invite this person to ask for help if there is a great deal to be read and outlined. Have another consult with the librarian and available bibliographies about additional publications which should be borrowed or purchased from other sources. Assign a third to examine business directories for a list of companies which should be visited or queried by letter. Ask a fourth to compile from directories a list of associations and similar nonpublic agencies to whom inquiries might be addressed. Send a fifth to talk with your municipal legal counsel—or a private attorney who's willing to provide advice—for a review of legal technicalities and requirements related to your venture. Ask others to interview all relevant local officials and agencies. Engage one person in correspondence with your congressman, and send another to see your state legislator; these officials are your best sources of guidance to national and state agencies which may have information, ideas, or even potential financial support for your project. And by all means, give at least one person the job of consulting the U.S. Government Printing Office—the world's largest publishing enterprise, concerned primarily with public problems and affairs.

A few massive directories—all generally available in well-stocked public libraries—will be particularly helpful in identifying sources of information. The subject guide volume of *Books in Print* (published by R. R. Bowker Company) attempts to list by subject category all books currently available from American publishers. *Ulrich's International Periodicals Directory*, also published by R. R. Bowker Company, describes magazines and specialized journals from all over the world by reasonably detailed subject categories, with excellent price indexes and addresses of publishers. *The Reader's Guide to Periodical Literature* (compiled by the H. H. Wilson Co.) is a continuing index of articles about given subject which appear in a broad selection of leading magazines. There are many good directories of companies which provide specific types of products; one of the most extensive, useful, and generally available is the *Thomas Register of American Manufacturers,* published annually by Thomas Publishing Company.

Perhaps the best guide to nongovernmental professional, trade, and other special interest associations which might have useful information, ideas, and guidelines is *The Encyclopedia of Associations* (published by Gale Research Company). Volume I —"National Associations of the United States"—is organized by broad subject areas. Volume II is a geographic index with executive listings. Volume III is a cumulative listing of newly established associations. This encyclopedia can be used not only to request information or descriptive pricelists of available publications from the organizations listed; it also enables you to ask appropriate associations to provide membership lists when you wish to inquire about products or services available from a particular industry or profession. Another good source of such specialized membership lists is the *Guide to American Directories* (published by B. Klein & Co.). This guidebook (by subject or industry and by geographic areas) includes many organizations whose membership lists are available for purchase.

As your researchers pursue these sources, ask them to report back frequently (to the coordinator you've appointed from the steering committee) about additional sources which have been pointed out to them in interviews or responses to their letters, or which they have discovered while reading. Keep the steering committee busy recruiting additional researchers to follow up these further assignments. If there are institutions of higher education within or near your community, assign additional researchers to examine their faculty rosters, inquire about relevant specialists, and seek interviews with those specialists.

Perhaps the most difficult type of information to find— unless you're dealing with a very common problem—will be accounts of related experiences in other communities. Your best chance here is to keep asking everyone you interview or write to if they know of such communities and of specific people within them who might be willing to share their insights. If you identify such a community but find no personal contact, write to the mayor or the city council and ask if they have a published report you can buy or borrow; write to the newspapers in the area (for addresses, consult the annual yearbook published by *Editor & Publisher* magazine) and request back issues, clippings, or photocopies of their coverage of the project; or ask the community's Chamber of Commerce if it will provide the names and addresses of several people connected with the project who might be willing to describe their experience.

A common shortcoming of civic improvement organizations is that they tend to give themselves too little time to prepare for effective action. This process of collecting information is a case in point. Unless your project is a very simple one, you should allow two or three months for the gathering and assembling of ideas and data and the organization of the results into useful form.

Unless you've waited too late to start (in view of forth-coming elections or other deadlines), you should complete this research process, as nearly as possible, before the public an-nouncement of your proposal for community action. Otherwise your announcement will be followed by a long period of informa-tion gathering in which nothing positive seems (in the general public view) to be happening. This will create the impression that your project has bogged down, lacks forceful leadership, or has been unable to win enough adherents to proceed.

This is one reason why it was suggested earlier that you start recruiting researchers—and handing out the more obvious assignments—at that first meeting of your steering committee. Research can proceed simultaneously with the preliminary plan-ning efforts of the steering committee.

Scheduling the research project before formal organiza-tion also gives you an opportunity to look over the growing body of recruits this effort has involved—to see who produces and who doesn't, who is enthusiastic and who isn't. This provides a reservoir of proven candidates for key assignments later in the project.

Information which has merely been collected is, how-ever, of little use. It must first be organized into some coherent form so that you can compare responses from varied sources and find what you're looking for at any given time through an orderly reference system. This process of organization should also in-clude evaluation. Don't let your project be discredited by giving opponents opportunities to demonstrate that some of the in-formation you are providing for the public is questionable. Mili-tary intelligence specialists distinguish between "information" (unconfirmed evidence) and "intelligence" (what we are confi-dent we can accept as true and relevant). Make the same distinc-tion in your own research program by eliminating or qualifying everything that seems exaggerated, that is too vague, or that has not been substantiated by facts.

Once information-gathering assignments have been made and research recruits are at work, focus the attention of your steering committee's research coordinator on shaping the final product into its most useful form. Too often a great deal of collected information remains unused because it is too cumbersome; a number of individuals are going to need to be able to find facts on a variety of subjects in the eventual research report without having to conduct a separate research project just to find them.

At this point—as at others—you'll discover the enormous value of people who can write. Unless your research coordinator has this talent, encourage (or insist upon) the recruitment of a research editor, who will devise an organized structure for the information you are gathering, apply critical standards of evaluation before any bit of information is poured into that structure, and assign to other writers the translation of all information collected on certain topics into an orderly compilation of all that has been learned about each topic.

Just as your information gatherers provide a reservoir of future manpower for organizational assignments, your research report writers become a talent pool for later publicity and other writing assignments.

As an end product, you should aim for one well-organized, dependable document, properly indexed or sectionalized so that specific information can be found in a hurry. This document should be reproduced and made available to all who will speak, or prepare publicity, for the project. Nothing builds public confidence as rapidly as the ability to cite specific facts which demonstrate that you know what you're talking about and which indicate that prestigious authorities are in agreement with your position.

A more voluminous file of individual researchers' reports may be maintained, and extended position papers may be prepared to cope with complex arguments on specific aspects of the project. But do not let these cumbersome stacks of paper substitute for one comprehensive, well-organized, basic information document to which every spokesman can refer in every public discussion. People who ask questions in public meetings want answers then, and "I'll consult the files" is seldom accepted as a good answer.

This research project, possibly extending over several months, and potentially involving a score or more volunteers, may seem like a lot of work before you've even gotten your campaign off the ground. But it will have added greatly to the prospects of your venture by nourishing the interest and commitment of a number of useful recruits.

Even more importantly perhaps, it will have greatly enhanced the work of the steering committee by providing a maximum of insight at a stage at which plans can still be shaped to capitalize on that insight. For this reason it is essential that communication between the steering committee and the research team be maintained.

An excellent way to do this—at least once, and perhaps more often—is to give your fledgling organization a morale-building look at itself in full force by setting up a joint planning-research meeting for a full exchange of information and ideas. Such meetings will also give *you* an opportunity to practice one of the most critical skills of the community activist—conducting meetings—before you have to do it in the glare of possible opposition or obstruction, in a general public meeting.

Let us consider next, then, how leadership is exercised in the larger forum of a formal (even if private) meeting.

CHAPTER FOUR

How to conduct a meeting

A good meeting is a work of art.

Bringing your steering committee and your entire research team together once or twice for semi-private exchanges of information and ideas—before you've established a public organization—will help you polish this art. And polish it you should, for nothing aids or hinders an organized endeavor as much as the quality of its meetings. Here is where people become inspired by signs of sound leadership and visible progress —or disheartened by wasted time and effort.

But such a preorganizational meeting should be more than a "practice session." Here you can deal with such problems as early expenses—before a budget and fund-raising apparatus has been established—by such simple means as a modest assessment of participants or by merely passing the hat. Here you can see which members of your fledgling organization are enthusiastic, which are performing well, before you pick a slate of permanent officers. And here you can collect a variety of ideas to cope with any stumbling blocks the steering committee has encountered in its planning processes.

You've undoubtedly been to enough bad meetings—disorganized, indecisive, wandering, unproductive, and much too long—to prepare you for the special satisfaction that comes from conducting a group session which gets its job done effectively in a minimum of time and sends everybody home while they're still in good spirits.

Such a successful outcome is not a spontaneous happening. It requires some work *before* the meeting. But much of this work can be delegated to other individuals, whose preliminary efforts will save much time for the larger group by dispensing with basic problems or evaluations which would otherwise have to be thrashed out in the general meeting.

Perhaps your meeting has one specific purpose (in this preliminary case, an exchange of general information and ideas between the researchers and the steering committee). But once you've gone to the trouble of getting all of your recruits together, you should attempt to accomplish as much as possible (without unduly prolonging the meeting). The more you get done in any meeting, the fewer meetings you'll have to have. Remember, every such meeting eats up volunteer man-hours which could otherwise be used in campaigning directly for your ultimate objective.

So in planning your meeting, consider what secondary purposes might also be accomplished. There are five general purposes for meetings, several of which are usually involved in any meeting you conduct:

(1) Meetings are vehicles for disseminating information; (2) meetings are mechanisms for making decisions, usually by placing the authority of the group behind appropriate, prepared proposals; (3) meetings serve to identify willing volunteers and facilitate the division of the group's workload through individual assignments; (4) meetings are a source of new ideas and insights when a diverse group of people direct their attention to a common problem; (5) meetings are occasions for organizational morale building by demonstrating to each participant the support which others are lending to his or her efforts.

In the case of this preorganizational meeting to get acquainted and exchange information, final decision making will hardly be appropriate. That must be left to the public meeting at which the organization is formalized, so that all who wish to participate can have a voice in the decisions. You will, in fact, unnecessarily encumber your steering committee just by allowing this broader meeting to dictate what that committee is to include in its proposals to the eventual public organizational meeting.

However, to make this preliminary meeting a helpful dress rehearsal for later gatherings—and to sharpen its focus—you might well ask for straw votes—nonbinding expressions of group sentiment—on key questions, to give the steering committee a more accurate measurement of the group's attitudes.

In many ways, then, this preliminary meeting will present the same problems and opportunities for its leadership—you—as any later, public meeting of your organization. The suggestions which follow will be equally applicable to this special type of meeting and to most subsequent meetings required by your campaign.

The first requirement for a good meeting is good attendance. Nothing disheartens an organization as rapidly as the feeling that few people are interested in its cause—that the workload will have to be borne by a small number of individuals; well-attended meetings provide instant proof that these negative conditions do not exist.

Until people get deeply involved in the work of an organization, their interest is very casual. They forget dates; they allow inconsequential alternatives to keep them away; they view your announced meeting as only one of several possibilities for the use of an evening, a lunch hour, or any other appointed time.

Once your meetings become public affairs, you will want to make maximum use of publicity channels—the press, posters, etc.—to promote attendance. But in this preorganizational stage —when you are still discreetly shielding your intentions from potential opponents—this task of promoting full attendance will have to be done more personally. This is the first task you should delegate to one or more of your associates. (This assignment can be used as training, to prepare one of your steering committee members for the bigger job of obtaining maximum attendance at your eventual public organizational meeting.)

Make sure that each individual is invited far enough in advance to prevent conflicts on their own calendars. Written notices are best; this reduces the chances of misunderstanding dates, places, etc. Then see that each invitation is followed up with a phone call a day or so before the meeting to make it obvious that you are anticipating each individual's presence. The actual process of last-minute telephone reminders can be delegated to a number of people, who in the process of urging others to attend will, in most cases, convince themselves.

In fact, it's a good idea to delegate preparatory assignments to as many people as possible—particularly those whose participation you consider most essential—so they'll have specific obligations to fulfill at the meeting. The task which can be most effectively delegated without losing control of the direction of the meeting is the presentation of background information on specific agenda items. Your research team will find such assignments both appropriate and (because of their research) reasonably easy.

You can multiply the number of people whose presence can be insured by such informational assignments by inviting panels of three or four people to speak briefly on the informational aspects of major agenda items. The invitation becomes subtle flattery because it designates these individuals as quasi-experts.

Delegating arrangements for refreshments is also a good way to give several people a specific obligation to attend. But consider serving the refreshments during the meeting rather than before or after. People who are reluctant to devote their leisure time to the business at hand will be even less enthusiastic about spending an additional half hour doing homage to a refreshment committee.

So much for attendance. The second essential ingredient of a good meeting is a clearly stated outline of what you hope to accomplish. This should be supported by a brief review of the group's authority—a reminder of what the meeting can, and cannot, properly attempt to decide. This latter consideration may depend on the stage of organization, on some public mandate (such as a petition), or on legal considerations (when you are following set procedures to influence public policy, as, for instance, in an election campaign).

This statement of the meeting's objective and authority should be made by you, the chairman, at the very beginning. But it should not be prepared until you have compiled and organized your agenda—so that it will be consistent with what is actually to follow.

The preparation of the list of agenda should be shared with your entire steering committee. But exercise certain discipline yourself—for instance, by seeing that items are inserted for the accomplishment of significant side benefits (such as morale building) when you see how this can be done in very little additional time, or by seeing that items are arranged in efficient order.

The key to efficient order is usually to present the simplest items first. The limited background discussion they require will begin to prepare the audience for more complex matters to follow. By the time you have reached your more complicated points, a broad spectrum of background information will have probably already been shared by the group.

If any topic could lead to a decision which would require additional money, manpower, or organization, follow it with an agenda item which will provide means of obtaining or creating these follow-up resources.

Some provision should be made for the addition of new items to the agenda after a meeting has begun. However, you should take simple precautions to prevent this exercise from getting out of hand—from overburdening a meeting with too much to do or from railroading proposals through a meeting without sufficient preparatory consideration.

The easiest way to do this is to make the first item of business after your general statement of purpose an "agenda report." Have someone from the steering committee actually present the prepared agenda (in brief, one-sentence-per-topic form) and make a motion that it be accepted as the official program for the meeting. Then invite additions (or deletions) in the form of amendments to the acceptance motion. Encourage other members of your steering committee to give assurance that new topics proposed on the spot will be considered in preparing the agenda for a future meeting if it seems desirable to delay action, or if too many amendments threaten to draw the meeting out to unreasonable length. In fact, you may want to include in your eventual by-laws a provision that new items cannot be added to a preannounced agenda until the next meeting, except under emergency provisions calling for general consensus rather than a simple majority vote.

When you and/or your steering committee draw up a proposed agenda in advance, you should include an informal timetable. This need not be included in your agenda report, but it will serve as a guide to you (the chairman) as to when you should speed up the discussion. Most meetings will gratefully accede to suggestions from the chair to conclude a discussion which is being unnecessarily prolonged. If they don't, your steering committee members should aid the chair by making motions to terminate or limit discussion.

To keep things moving, you and your steering committee should make certain in advance that two elements have been prepared for each topic on the agenda. The first is a background information report—a concise review of the facts the meeting will need to make a wise decision on the item in question. The second is a specific proposal for such action as you believe should be taken on the item. (In your preliminary planning-research meeting these will, of course, be only tentative proposals.) Certainly you will want to encourage alternate proposals from the meeting participants—and give these alternatives a fair chance for consideration and adoption—but you should never depend on a meeting to produce a spontaneous proposal for a course of action. Unless you have a good proposal waiting in the wings—in the hands of the steering committee, or the individual who presented the background information on the subject—either of two undesirable things is likely to happen: (1) the meeting will waste time fumbling for a feasible course of action, or (2) it will quickly adopt the first feasible suggestion made, without any balanced consideration of possibly more effective alternatives.

Finally, your agenda should include a provision for assigning specific people to undertake the tasks agreed upon by the meeting (either by on-the-spot volunteers or appointments, or by assuring the group of follow-up action by outlining the delegating process the chairman intends to exercise after the meeting). And you should always include a specific item—as the last order of business—to arrange for the conditions (and if feasible, the time and the place) for the next meeting. Never leave your organization hanging in mid-air in a way which will require you to repeat all the work of starting things up anew.

Along with the preparation of this agenda, you should consider the parliamentary procedure by which you are going to control the meeting. It is commonplace for organizations to include in their by-laws the adoption of some general, traditional parliamentary code (such as Roberts' *Rules of Order*). However, few of the participants in any meeting are going to study such manuals thoroughly and they will consequently disrupt your meeting with actions which are out of order, even when they are not trying to be disruptive.

The simplest way around this complication is to provide a brief outline of general rules of procedure, and then state that the chair will take the prerogative of keeping things moving and keeping the group from digressing beyond the subject at hand, subject to being overruled at any time by a majority of the participants. This means simply that the chairman runs the meeting as he or she sees fit until and unless someone objects to any action from the chair—at which point the group quickly (and without debate) decides whether to overrule or support the chairman's decision.

If you take this approach, keep the rules simple. Begin with adoption or amendment of the prepared agenda; take each item in order; accept (for a group vote) motions to limit or end discussion at any time; encourage such motions whenever the meeting lags behind your tentative timetable; confine each agenda item to two forms of discussion: (1) the presentation of relevant reports—such as the background information reports you have assigned specific individuals to prepare, or subcommittee reports; (2) further discussion *only* on motions for specific action to be taken in regard to the topic at hand. Do not allow broad, generalized discussion which goes beyond the motion on the floor at the time. Remember that only one motion (and amendments thereto) can be under consideration at any given time—and that the only ways to dispose of a motion are by: (1) voting on it; (2) voting on a secondary motion to table it or delay action until a specific future date; (3) allowing the individual who made the motion— and any required seconders—to withdraw it in the light of subsequent discussion.

It is customary that the chair not accept any motion for consideration until it has been seconded by someone other than its originator. This is a device which saves the group the time required to get obviously ridiculous or inappropriate notions off the floor. (There is no reason why you can't write into your eventual by-laws a provision requiring even more than one seconder —but this is a safeguard normally employed only for very large meetings, subject to a wide variety of extraneous influences.)

Once you've prepared your agenda (perhaps an hour's thoughtful work for you or your steering committee), fixed your rules of procedure firmly in your own mind (and perhaps incorporated them in your opening statement, if this is the first meeting of the group), assigned specific people to present background information on each item, made certain that somebody has ready a specific proposal for such action as should be taken on each item, and assigned specific responsibilities for the task of getting an appropriate audience to attend—you're all set to conduct a meeting which will give you the same kind of satisfaction a drama enthusiast receives from directing an outstanding stage play.

But remember that you are more than the director of the performance which is going to follow; you are the central figure in the cast, yet you do not want to be the obvious "star." Your mission is to draw other people out of their shells—or their seats —and get them to perform. The amount of participation you can provoke—without prolonging the meeting or letting it get out of control—will be a direct measure of the democratic health of your organization and the commitment and morale of its adherents.

There's no reason to be nervous; you have a script (your agenda outline) to follow. Ideally, you should say as little as possible once the meeting has begun; but you should be as firm as you are brief in your interventions to keep the discussion moving—and on target.

Make yourself comfortable; there's no reason why a chairman shouldn't remain seated, as long as everyone can see him (or her) clearly. Be sure you have some means of demanding the group's attention when you wish to intervene; that's what gavels are for, but if a gavel is too pretentious for your style, keep your eye on an empty (and durable) ash tray.

Make sure you can see everyone; spread the participation by recognizing first those who want to speak and have not yet played an active part in the discussion; don't be bashful about interrupting and discouraging that inevitable fellow who revels in the sound of his own voice by dominating the discussion of every item. And look for those fidgety, shy people whose gestures indicate they'd like to speak but who haven't mustered the courage to raise their hands. It is not only proper but wise to invite them to take the floor by simply asking: "Were you about to say something?"

And when you get to the end of the agenda, don't wait for other people to "run down" and call for adjournment. Once the tasks created by the meeting have been assigned, or provisions for later delegation have been announced, and the conditions of the next meeting have been determined, *invite* a motion to end it. ("Does the chair hear a motion for adjournment?")

Now that we've been through a tight procedure for brisk and effective meetings, we should consider one exception which violates most of the rules we've established. There come times in all organizations—and particularly in very crucial meetings—when participants need to clear the air of concerns which do not fit directly into the discussion of any specific action item. In other words, sometimes people *do* need to digress—to talk things over generally without the pressure of proposing specific action motions in advance.

A very simple and widely used procedure can accomplish this. When you sense such an occasion, invite a motion to recess the meeting to a committee of the whole for a certain number of minutes.

A committee of the whole consists of the same people engaged in the regular meeting but reverts by agreement back to the preparatory level of the steering committee, where discussion is informal and generalized. This means that anybody can say anything—the chairman relinquishing control of the agenda—for the agreed period of time. Then the chairman calls the recess to an end, reconvenes the formal meeting, and proceeds with the agenda item interrupted by the recess motion.

This may seem an unnecessarily formal device. Why not just let the meeting wander off the subject for awhile?

The problem with such informality is that the chairman gives up control without any understood means of regaining it. You may then have to ruffle feathers and stifle enthusiasms to get things back on the track. And digression without such a formal agreement as "recessing to a committee of the whole" may irritate those impatient participants who are depending on you to get them home before the babysitter's rates go up.

There will be occasions, of course, in which you'll turn large portions of a meeting over to other people—for instance, to a panel moderator who will lead a special discussion. In such cases it is a good idea to agree in advance how long these inter- ruptions of your control will last (even in the case of giving the floor to someone for a report, unless you know they'll be prop- erly brief). Don't let someone else ruin your meeting by keeping a restless audience silent and uninvolved for too long.

The types of meetings which you must conduct in leading any project to success will vary—from small, informal committee work sessions to mass rallies. Generally speaking, however, the procedures we've just reviewed will provide a structure for any such group. An hour of preparation on your part (within or with- out a steering committee) and assignment of specific, equally brief tasks to a few of your colleagues can cut far more than an hour off the time required for a general meeting.

And even more importantly, such preparation will result in a productive meeting—one which will impress the public with your prospects for eventual success, and build enthusiasm among participants who experience this living evidence that their efforts are going to lead to action.

Nothing will confirm your own role as a leader—and induce others to follow you—as quickly or decisively as a good performance behind the gavel. And nothing will insure such a per- formance as readily as a modest amount of orderly pre-meeting preparation.

Perhaps the semi-private, preliminary meeting you've called to exchange views between the steering committee and the researchers will require only a small part of the detailed proce- dures outlined above. But consider them all in planning that meeting—get the entire task of controlling a flexible gathering well fixed in your mind. For future meetings will, possibly, offer a challenging new dimension which this friendly gathering did not have—opposition. Before you face it, get as firm a grasp as pos- sible on these procedures for maintaining control.

It is, however, not just in meetings that potential oppo- nents can complicate your campaign problems. Let us turn now to a consideration of such opposition and how it will affect your organization.

CHAPTER FIVE

Hostility control

People who try to change things frequently find themselves the objects of hostile community reaction. Some of this hostility will be logically expressed—and directed toward the proposal you're supporting rather than the people who are supporting it (i.e., objections to costs and other factual aspects of your program). This sort of opposition is the legitimate form of public debate and will neither surprise nor disturb your campaigners.

But much of the hostility your proposal arouses will be more emotional and less logical. It may take the form of angry invective or, at the very least, unfair innuendos. Your innovative campaigners will be labeled "troublemakers"—with the insinuation that they have gone beyond the limits of conventional respectability.

Fear of such hostility can dissuade many potential recruits from joining your cause. Demagogic exploitation of the strong emotions it arouses will assist your opponents in marshaling people and resources to combat your efforts. And no matter how unfair or untrue the insinuations of your detractors may be, they will leave the public with an unpleasant aftertaste which will penalize your cause whenever the indifferent and the uninformed cast their votes or voice their casual opinions.

But what can you do about it, other than steering clear of controversial proposals—a limitation which may well make it impossible to attack basic community problems?

The first thing you can do, as we've suggested earlier, is to make sure you aren't giving potential opponents any unnecessary advantages by exposing your plans prematurely. Many people never progress beyond the first impressions they form of an idea or an organization or an individual, such as a political candidate. It is important that before you expose your campaign to attack, you be prepared with the information, the arguments, and the arrangement of a public forum which will put your case before the community in the best possible light.

This means not tipping your hand in preliminary information-seeking interviews with public agencies. Don't tell them you're alarmed about a problem; ask if they think one exists. Don't tell them what you're considering doing about it; ask what they think might be done.

One of the major causes of official hostility to citizen-proposed innovations is the implication that the officials haven't been doing their job properly. This attitude is often apparent when a citizen group calls on a public agency or officer. And too often it causes unnecessary complications.

So while being discreet, you might also try giving the public officials you and your information gatherers interview an opportunity to be "good guys" before you drive them into the opposition with criticism—open or implied.

When an official exhibits real concern about the problem you have in mind, encourage him to talk about solutions. Urge him to elaborate on any suggestions which are compatible with the course of action you are planning. If his interest seems sincere, you might even invite him to present his ideas before your steering committee or research team; but introduce your group merely as an "informal committee investigating what might be done about the problem" rather than as an action organization, which it has yet to become.

The ultimate success with this technique of hostility control is to get a public official to believe that he has actually inspired much of the concern you will later express to the public. He may well back away when the arguments start, but he will almost certainly have been neutralized from joining the active opposition.

But the most serious wave of public hostility you can expect to face will come immediately after your first public announcement of the innovation you seek to bring about. The implications of your proposal are still largely unknown, and people react suspiciously and usually negatively to the unknown (particularly in the area of tax-supported public services).

It is important to remember that these first reactions may prejudice many people so strongly that it will be impossible to change their minds later. And if the public hostility is widespread and strongly expressed, it will seriously hamper your recruiting efforts at exactly the stage when they should be yielding their greatest results.

So make certain that your publicity machinery (see Chapters Six and Eleven) is in good order—prepared to get your public campaign started in a favorable light—before you stage your public announcement. And stress that verb "stage"; treat the initial announcement as a dramatic production—and milk it for every good impression possible.

To do this, you'll need to arrange a forum which will attract wide attention. You might literally create a news event—for example, by inviting a number of prestigious community leaders (including sympathetic public officials) to discuss the problem you've documented as members of a panel—and announce your project during that open discussion. The prestigious personalities will add little to what you already know—if you've done your homework—but they'll lend your enterprise some respectability by association.

You might conduct a tour, exhibiting obviously bad conditions which you hope to improve and producing some photographs which local newspapers will find it hard to resist—making sure some well-known and highly respected community leaders are included in the photographs and identified with your cause. Present your formal announcement to the press with the photographs.

The most popular forum-producing, publicity-winning device of recent years has been the protest demonstration. Such demonstrations have one effect which you'll generally want to avoid at this early stage of your enterprise: they goad your potential opponents as well as your supporters into action because they make people involve themselves emotionally in the questions you're posing for the community. Before your project slips into such a complex confrontation, be sure you've thought it through. But in the last analysis, don't dismiss the protest (be it angry or merely satirical) as a device for awaking public concern and creating press and political attention, when other methods have failed because of apathy.

Whatever device you decide to employ for drawing press and public attention to your announcement, make sure that your announcement statement contains all that you can pack into it for the purpose of anticipating and disarming opposition. If the project is going to cost public money (or even if it is a cooperative and you're opening a drive for private contributions or investments), try to translate the benefits which will result into monetary terms to demonstrate that it is a good bargain. (Try to show how continuation of the problem could cost the community far more than your solution would cost.) Give a sufficient description of your informal group, including as many highly reputed names as possible, to head off charges that you are irresponsible or insignificant troublemakers. (Socially conscious clergymen can make a particularly helpful impression for you.)

Spell out the motives, the background facts, the costs, and the benefits. Outline enough of your project to demonstrate that it is feasible. But *don't* outline detailed plans for putting the project across if you anticipate any opposition. Why make it easy for opponents to counter your moves?

Once you have presented your case before the public in a manner calculated to head off the most blatant attackers, try neutralizing particularly important, potentially hostile, officials and community leaders. Recruit people who are on friendly, somewhat intimate terms with such individuals to conduct interviews with them, directly asking for their support. This probably won't change anyone's mind, but it will tend to neutralize opposition by making these prospective opponents hesitant about flinging unfair accusations at people they know, people who have shared certain confidences with them.

Yet no matter how carefully you stage the presentation of your project, you're going to get under somebody's skin. When the public arguments start, remember that no matter what is being said, the side whose position is being argued over is usually the winner. To attack what you are proposing, your opponents must help you make the community aware of that proposal; certainly they'll put it in an unfavorable light, but they're not going to convince as many people as they inform.

So, as far as possible, refrain from any direct reaction to the opposition; pretend they don't exist; build positive answers to their criticisms into your subsequent publicity—but do it subtly and gently, without appearing to accept those criticisms as significant. In brief, concentrate your discussion on *your* case, not the opposition's, and thus force the opposition to help you inform the public about your case if they wish a context for attacking it.

When face-to-face debate situations do arise (you'll want to discourage them if you think you're ahead in the contest, since they'll only provide equal time to help the opposition catch up), "play it cool." Follow the same tactics; concentrate on your message rather than the opposition's. Answer critical questions as briefly and factually as possible, and then get back to your own arguments.

Don't hesitate to remind your organization that the opposition will use any opportunity it can to discredit you because of the manner in which you campaign. Some people become involved in projects like yours to find an arena for working out their personal hostilities and hang-ups. Friends like that you can do without.

Think about those college kids who went out in the winter and spring of 1968—when the public image of youthful activists was at a low point because of conventional displeasure over draft protests and hippies and the LSD kick—and came within a respectable distance of winning a presidential nomination for Senator Eugene McCarthy. McCarthy could have multiplied his army of youthful campaigners by inviting every segment of teenage protest to come forth and do its thing. But the senator's campaign directors had the courage to attach a condition.

This condition was summarized by the slogan "Clean for Gene." McCarthy's recruiters pointed out that it could not advance their cause to ridicule universal values which had nothing to do with the campaign by confronting ordinary citizens with blatant reminders of what disturbed them about youthful protest. They insisted on neatness, discouraged beards, encouraged good manners. And those polite young people who responded won the McCarthy campaign many thousands of votes—and saved it millions of dollars—by simply reassuring the public that some of their fonder images of youth were still valid.

If teen-agers can do it, certainly adults can. Remind your colleagues as often as necessary that their objective is to win public support, not to "tell anyone off" or get their own indignation and frustration out of their systems.

But you should also point out that however carefully you prepare and however well you behave, some opponents will still deal roughly with you. Changes in a community disturb vested interests, by means which vary from the creation of public competition for private businesses, to the rerouting of traffic through previously quiet neighborhoods. No amount of tact, no barrage of facts will make those who stand to lose money (or power, or prestige) like your venture—or even be reasonable and courteous in their criticism of it, and of its adherents.

We've concerned ourselves here with minimizing early hostility which can impede recruiting. In Chapter Nine we'll consider ways of helping recruits overcome the effects of hostility when campaigning. Meanwhile, don't create the illusion that you can eliminate all hostility. Remind your fellow campaigners that political activity is one of the nearest approaches we have to the "moral equivalent of war" which William James once envisioned as a substitute for our military instincts.

Facing inescapable hostility well—learning to channel one's own responses constructively—will be one of the most gratifying personal experiences you can promise those who join your cause.

CHAPTER SIX

Creating the right
first impression in public

You've undoubtedly noticed that before any competent politician formally announces his or her candidacy for a major post, the potential candidate becomes highly visible through "nonpolitical" speaking engagements, personal sponsorship of a spate of legislation, magazine articles or interviews, or possibly a well-publicized trip abroad. You've seen how congressional committees use public investigations to create general concern about problems before they introduce their proposed solutions.

These preliminary maneuvers have the same function as a peacock's tail feathers. They are designed to capture the attention of an audience before which the politician (or the peacock) is about to make a proposition and to influence that audience to be favorably disposed.

The results of your preliminary research program can be, for your project, what those beautiful tail feathers are to the peacock. Whether you've come up with inspiring possibilities or only with shocking documentation that "we got trouble right here in River City," you now have a body of information which no one else could duplicate—or fully answer—without the same extensive effort and advance planning which your group devoted to developing it. In the week or two before you spring your proposal on the community, this information can be used to make sure people are listening when you do proposition them.

And if you've been reasonably discreet in your research interviews, no one will be prepared to talk back. You have perhaps ten days of more or less uncontested opportunity to "stack the deck" by making sure that the public's first general impressions are those which will best support your eventual appeal for broad public support.

It is important that you plan to do this just *before* your public organizational meeting, and the announcement of your specific proposal. In the first place, the attendant publicity will help you get an audience to that organizational meeting. Secondly, by getting there first with your version of the facts you will have established the lines along which future opponents will have to argue—because you will have implanted certain questions or conditions in the public mind, which any opponent will have to surmount or circumvent before attempting to lead public opinion in a different direction. Thirdly, you will have wiped out some of the natural suspicion of troublemakers by demonstrating that a problem exists, before you tax people to align themselves with an effort to change things. And finally, responses to this preliminary release of information—before battle lines are drawn around specific proposals—will help you assess which community leaders are potentially with you, and which will become probable obstacles.

Just as you assigned research coordination to one specific member of your steering committee, you should delegate this task of using that research to set the stage for your organizational meeting to another member. And you should do it early in the game—when your research effort is just getting underway—so the assigned coordinator can make careful plans well in advance, and constantly adjust those plans to achieve the greatest possible impact from each major research finding.

This coordinator will want to study Chapter Eleven to anticipate certain aspects of the eventual organizational publicity program. A few additional advance recruits may be needed. But by using the research team, the writers it will inevitably need, and the spokesmen which exist in the steering committee, a one- or two-week burst of preliminary publicity should be attainable without an extensive organization or apparatus.

It is unwise to begin leaking information through this brief campaign too soon. While it won't reveal your specific plans, the preliminary campaign will certainly alert potential opponents to the fact that you have some serious intentions—and allow them to begin marshaling defenses. Furthermore, if the preliminary information campaign is too long, the public will begin to get bored; even though you haven't launched your actual project, the public will get the impression that you have—and draw negative conclusions from the fact that no specific accomplishments are being made.

There are a number of ways of feeding the information—the documentation of a problem—which you have gathered into the arena of public attention. You may want to combine several. But don't overextend yourself; remember, you're still an informal organization with limited manpower. Put together a feasible plan for advance publicity and then concentrate on carrying it out like clockwork, rather than diffusing it to cover all possibilities.

Remember that one object of this advance publicity is to produce a crowd for your forthcoming organizing meeting. Announcing this meeting serves notice on potential objectors that you do have some serious action intentions, whether they can deduce specifically what they are or not. So in this advance publicity stage, you need to plan carefully to achieve maximum publicity for the initial organizational meeting while giving the potential opposition as little time as possible to take countermeasures.

To accomplish this, avoid all mention of a forthcoming organizational meeting while you are making arrangements with the press or with other organizations for your advance information forum. Do not announce the organizational meeting in your first public release. But immediately thereafter include the time and place and general purpose of the meeting in all subsequent releases. If your initial revelation of a community problem has made news, this further indication that someone is preparing to do something about it will be an essential follow-up story that the press will be unlikely to ignore.

Now then, what specific devices can you use to generate public awareness and concern before you organize and make your specific proposition?

If your community has its own newspaper or radio station, your task should be relatively easy. If it doesn't, you'll have to build in enough drama to interest the regional press.

Perhaps your documentation of a problem or your outline of an unachieved community opportunity will be striking enough to engage the press on its own merits. But even if it isn't, the impact of such serious citizen concern about a public matter on the community's political status quo will be obvious to the press; without taking sides, they'll generally welcome the opportunity to demonstrate that they were among the first to know something was in the wind.

Perhaps the simplest way to deal with the press would be to present your complete research report to every news medium which covers your community. But this has three disadvantages: it shoots all of your ammunition in the first salvo, instead of using it to get repetitive public attention over a number of days; it confronts the press with a great deal of work, digesting and summarizing the report, and, like other people, newsmen are more receptive to what is easy than to what is hard; and it eliminates the possibility of arranging related dramas which could heighten public interest.

To get the most mileage out of your research report, you should relate it to several consecutive news events; you should use it in a way which involves people other than your informal group; and you should provide the press with precondensed material appropriate to each event. For example:

(1) Pick an official public agency relevant to your project—perhaps the school committee if you're tackling teen-age drug use, or the housing authority if you're campaigning for low-cost housing. Have your spokesman phone the chairman in advance, as a private citizen, and ask permission to present some information of public interest at its next meeting (being as unspecific as possible). A few hours before the meeting, have notes hand-delivered to each local news medium indicating that private citizens are about to enliven an official meeting with some startling information; this should either get them there or make them receptive to your own report of what happened. At that meeting, unload the most sensational items from your research report, and have extra copies available for the press. If the press doesn't attend, write your own news story dramatizing the presentation, and deliver it immediately after the meeting (along with the de-

scription of the research items you unveiled) to every local news medium. Story #1.

(2) At that public meeting, have your spokesman conclude his revelations by stating that several private citizens have collected a great deal of additional information, and would like to present it in organized form to the public official who could best suggest what they might do about it. Make an appointment right then and there for such a presentation several days hence. If you're asked to turn it over on the spot, insist that it isn't quite complete. (You want a separate occasion for the full presentation —for additional news coverage.) Keep that later appointment, and, if possible, supplement the copy of the full report which you present by photographs demonstrating the condition you hope to change. Immediately after your interview, deliver copies of the full report—and the photographs—to all local news media, with a cover story describing the interview factually. Story #2.

(3) Two or three days after this interview, prepare a straightforward announcement (with covering news story) of your forthcoming organizational meeting—referring back to previous news stories to illustrate the need for the meeting. Include in this announcement the statement that a full, documented report on the problem has been presented to all local news media—to encourage them to publish it (or substantial portions of it) as proof that they aren't slighting the problem. Story #3.

Instead of, or in addition to, this staged unveiling of the full report as a build-up for announcing your organizational meeting, you might prepare a series of articles and offer them to the local press. Your best chance to get them used is to offer one news medium an exclusive, though if you have several local media, this might prejudice the others against you; in that case, make sure you've picked the most effective one.

In the case of a radio station, you might describe how your research team has operated, and offer one or several of its members for a broadcast interview, or series of interviews. Or you might propose yourself or another spokesman as a guest on one of those radio talk shows, which feature telephone conversations with listeners about topics of public interest and arouse a good deal of local discussion.

Another approach involves using a variety of existing local organizations as forums. Program chairmen are constantly in need of speakers or panels. If you plan it a month or two in advance, you can offer every such organization in your community a very revealing program, simply by stating that several responsible citizens are now investigating such-and-such an obvious problem and would be willing to present what they learn at the organization's next meeting.

The trick here is to work well in advance to get invitations to make the presentation at several such meetings during a brief period, shortly before your anticipated organizational meeting. But don't scare people off by presenting your offer as a prelude to an organizing effort that may well have strong partisan overtones. In fact, don't mention the organizational meeting at the first several such gatherings; wait until you've created some public notice of the problem; but keep notes of particularly interested people you encounter in all such meetings, and see that they get special invitations once the organizational meeting is announced.

If you use this approach, don't ignore the press—and don't leave it to the press to do its own work in covering the programs at which you or your colleagues perform. In the best journalistic style your writer-recruits can muster, prepare a news story covering each appearance and deliver it to every local news medium. (Don't deliver advance announcements of your appearances, however; this may seem "pushy" to your host organization —and create unnecessary tensions before you've accomplished your purpose.)

If your community is small, you can stir interest on a more personal basis—and learn who should be invited to the organizational meeting—by using your steering committee and your research crew to conduct a house-to-house survey. It isn't necessary to cover the entire community, but the more people you contact, the more effective this approach will be.

Prepare a questionnaire which does not put the respondent on the spot by making him say what he'll do about the problem, but merely asks (in several ways) whether he agrees that a problem exists, and perhaps how he ranks several alternative solutions. Along with the questionnaire, prepare a very brief statement (perhaps half a page) of the most compelling background facts your researchers have unearthed. Assign each individual surveyor a specific area; have them ring doorbells and say: "Would you mind reading this brief description of a community problem and answering a few survey questions about it?" Assure them that their names will not be used in reporting the survey results.

If the survey produces striking results, you have a good opportunity to prepare a news story which can be delivered to the press along with your full research report. And if you'll ask enough qeustions, you'll get striking results of some kind or other. If people express general concern, there's your story. If they don't, use the survey to document lack of public awareness of a problem which you can clearly demonstrate, and make that your story.

Be prepared to cover a good portion of the community with the survey itself, by pouring all of your manpower into it. Make sure each canvasser takes notes of individual reactions; you don't even have to inhibit people by asking their names to do this; use street lists or phone books to determine (by addresses and sex) to whom you were probably talking. You'll be right 95 per cent of the time. Or have canvassers check the names from such lists in advance, and identify the individuals as they answer the door: "Mrs. Jones?" If it happens to be Mrs. Jones's mother-in-law, she'll accept the mistake as natural and correct you.

In the course of these interviews, you'll be able to identify people who share your concern and may be willing to work with you. These are the people you'll want to concentrate on when getting out invitations to your organizational meeting. And, needless to say, such interviews—if carried out on a broad scale —will be very educational for your core leadership group, the steering committee, and research team members who are conducting the survey.

But whatever you learn from the answers, keep remembering that the real object is to get a lot of people to read your brief background statement. Whether or not they agree to answer your questions, or show any interest in aiding your cause, every person who reads that half page has been effectively conditioned for your later efforts to create strong public opinion.

Some of these preliminary maneuvers may be easier if you constitute your original recruits as a temporary, semi-formal organization—to make people less suspicious, to give the press a "handle" with which to discuss your efforts. If so, don't use a name which suggests that you're already committed to a course of action—or even to taking action. Call it a "citizens' study committee" or a "public information committee."

The existence of such a temporary entity can enable you to use other preliminary publicity devices which don't require an established forum. For example, such a committee might organize guided tours of problem areas—to demonstrate housing or traffic problems, to display youngsters conducting games in dangerous streets for lack of recreational facilities, to visit inadequate institutions or facilities. You can't expect such tours to intrigue large portions of the community; they're too much trouble for those not yet committed. So you should concentrate on turning them into appealing news features for local media.

The easiest way to do this to take prestigious people with you; if you can persuade the mayor to join you on such a tour in order to provide specific examples supplementing your research report, you're almost certain to get news coverage. But short of this, assemble every more or less sympathetic local celebrity you can—and see that the press is invited.

But again, don't peg everything on the willingness of the press to cover your tour. Make sure you have a good photographer along, and provide pictures for every medium which can use them. Write your own news stories for immediate delivery to every medium which wasn't represented.

Under the aegis of a temporary committee, you might also build your case by publishing a preorganizational newsletter. But don't think in terms of weeklies or monthlies; that exposes you too far in advance and gives you too few exposures; furthermore, yours becomes just one of many such occasional newsletters all public leaders and journalists receive.

Instead, do something that will jolt your audience; make it a daily release, coming to them out of the blue for the last ten or so days before your organizational meeting. Unfold your case day by day, and get gradually more specific about your intention to do something about it, by building up the details of your organizational meeting when it's too late for anyone to interfere. The press will be more responsive to such a newsletter if it is apparent that it is also going to concerned public officials; make sure you include some statement which indicates that this is so.

Don't worry about fancy production; a mimeograph or spirit duplicator will do very well. But *don't* send carbon or photocopied newsletters; this makes it too obvious that very few people are receiving your releases. You'll get more reaction from both officials and the press if they suspect you might be generally propagandizing the community.

In presenting these approaches to preliminary publicity, we've purposefully slighted the one most often used—and the one which might seem most obvious and reasonable to you. Why not just call a big public meeting a week before your organizational meeting, spread all your facts on the table, and invite those who share your concerns to come back next week and set up an organization?

The first problem with this approach is that it constitutes an awful lot of work: you'll have to produce a very large audience to have enough left for an organization after the disinterested are weeded out. Furthermore, a small audience will create the impression—both publicly and within your group—that there's little interest in the subject, and this will cast a deadly pall over your subsequent organizational meeting.

If you should decide to package all of your preliminary publicity efforts into one such meeting, be prepared to spend some money advertising it through local news media; you need to get the idea before the public more often than in the one advance story they may give you. And pull out all the stops in keeping all of your original recruits busy phoning everyone they know.

An intensive two-week campaign, then—one which documents and dramatizes the problem you hope to solve, without revealing how you plan to solve it—will not only help produce an interested audience for your organizational meeting; it will provide a generally acceptable rationale for that meeting. The public will see you forming an organization in response to a problem which already exists, rather than suspecting you of dredging up a problem just to give your organization a cause. And your preliminary revelations will have anticipated the opposition by planting in the public mind—while the whole subject is still an interesting novelty—the key facts and questions which will be hardest for your opponents to surmount.

But unless you've achieved epic publicity successes (which are rare), you'll still find the public cautious and slow-moving. You may have proved that something *needs* to be done, but you'll still find that most people won't commit themselves until they're also convinced that something *can* be done—in a reasonable time, without unreasonable demands on them.

Thus it would seem that the next step is to get organized —to start doing. But remember that the next great impression the public forms of your venture will be whether or not it is making progress, proving itself feasible.

So even before you unwind your preliminary publicity, you should be prepared to insure fast progress in and after the subsequent organizational meeting—a meeting which should follow close on the heels of the preliminary publicity, while you still have the public's attention.

The key to immediate progress is to make sure your advance planning has been completed in the soundest possible fashion. Now let's focus on the specific planning documents which can give you that assurance.

CHAPTER SEVEN

Timetables, organization, budgets, and by-laws

Once you've planned your campaign, set the stage for your public announcement, and prepared your organization for such hostility as can be anticipated, you're almost ready to share your plans with the world and start campaigning. But first, your steering committee must reduce what it has planned to such clear and unmistakable form that it can be easily understood, acted upon, and recorded as the basis of future campaign operations.

Generally speaking, four written documents will put into visible and usable form the basic planning details which a steering committee should complete before it goes out of business: a timetable, an organization chart, a budget, and a set of by-laws.

The discussions you've held to choose a basic plan—supplemented by the information your research team gathers—will have passed over most of the ground your detailed plan must cover. Feasible time spans, the functions which must be provided for in the organization chart, the magnitude of your budgetary requirements, the nature of your necessary by-laws will have become fairly obvious.

But a brief review of what each of these essential documents must cover will assist you in delegating their preparation to individual steering committee members and in making sure that the group's ultimate consideration of those individual proposals is sound.

A timetable (see Appendix III) is essentially a calendar of the anticipated career of your project. It forces you to organize your plans into an orderly and realistic sequence because it commits you to an estimate of over-all time which cannot be made until you've identified every work segment of the project.

This should be a real calendar, built around specific dates.

You start constructing it by identifying the inflexible dates which are significant to your project: petition-filing deadlines, election days, schedules for local government budget processes, critical points in the programs of other organizations which will become involved.

From each mandatory date which you thus place on the calendar, you must think backward to schedule the time necessary for each step you must take to prepare for that mandatory date. For example:

You intend to file a petition to your City Council asking that money to hire a specially qualified youth officer be added to its forthcoming police budget—the specific objective you've chosen to cope with the teen-age drug problem. The Council determines this budget at some indeterminant time in October. September 30 thus becomes a mandatory date for completing the collection of petition signatures. If you think it will take ten people a maximum of three weeks to collect the signatures you need, your signature drive will have to begin around September 7. The weekend before that is Labor Day weekend, and many potential workers will be away for the holiday, so your recruiting and orientation of the people who will collect the signatures must be completed by, say, August 31. You anticipate that within a week each of the five supervisors of your petition drive can recruit and instruct three canvassers, so recruiting must begin in earnest by August 24. It will take about a week to get the petition forms reproduced, and to instruct and supply (and aid in recruiting) the canvassers, so the petition must be in final form by about August 17. One of your members is prepared to write it in one weekend, but wants several days to check it with an attorney—so the first draft should be done around August 13.

Working backward from each inflexible date on your calendar thus becomes a simple disciplining factor in the development of your total plan. It will force you to make the strategic decisions early, rather than as last-minute snap judgments. For example, in working out the schedule above you have to decide whether you're going to collect only the minimum number of petition signatures legally required, or whether you're going to flood City Hall with thousands of voters' endorsements as a means of pressuring the Council to do what you want, because you cannot determine the time needed for signature collection or recruiting until you've decided how extensive your campaign will be. Or perhaps you're going to focus public opinion by first submitting a petition and then generating broad support for it to influence the Council—a course which would require submission of the petition well in advance of the Council's budget session, and to which you would have to be firmly committed before the calendar could be completed.

Consult a calendar which lists dates of religious significance, legal holidays, and public observances or anniversaries which could be related to your project. Which represent publicity opportunities? Which indicate dates on which many people will be unavailable—for meetings, for work, or in their homes where you hope to obtain their signatures or their attention?

Consult friends or clergymen to be certain your timetable will not offend the sacred observances of any faith. Make specific allowances for appropriate dates in the case of ethnic neighborhoods within the community.

Track down the regular meeting dates of other organizations which will overlap your membership—and avoid them for your meetings or work projects in order to insure maximum participation. Check major school and athletic events for the same purpose.

Remember that special observance dates may provide opportunities to attract attention to your project, if it is appropriate for your organization to participate in public ceremonies. And any scheduled community event which will collect a crowd offers you an opportunity for distributing literature, surveying opinions, or exhibiting displays. Those local politicians outside the gate at the high school homecoming football game are smart; they know it's easier to go to a crowd than to bring one to you.

Your timetable should indicate the interrelationships between various tasks which will be carried out more or less simultaneously. For instance:

*To increase the number of questionnaires your door-to-door
canvassers can collect during an opinion survey, you've decided to mail the questionnaires and background information in
advance, encouraging householders to fill them out and have them
ready when the canvassers call. You're going to print an information sheet, which will take ten days including typesetting, but the
questionnaire form itself will be mimeographed in the office of
one of your steering committee members, a one-hour task. It will
take two weeks to get the envelopes addressed by volunteers and
another week to get them stuffed and sealed and stamped. The
stationery store wants a week's advance notice to special order
the envelopes you'll need.*

*Quite obviously, the date of your door-to-door canvass
now depends more on the schedule for your mailing than it does
on the recruitment and orientation of canvassers. The first thing
you've got to do is order envelopes. Assuming three days between
mailing them and sending canvassers door-to-door to collect
them, you can't schedule your collection day until at least four
weeks and three days after you order the envelopes (one week
to get the envelopes, two for addressing, one for stuffing, three
days for postal delivery and householder consideration). Your
next task will be preparing the information sheet for the printer,
so he can have it ten days before envelope addressing is to be
completed. While the actual questionnaire may be the thing which
concerns you most, it can wait, since it can be done in one day
and won't be needed until three weeks after you order envelopes.*

The easiest way to bring such interrelated schedules into
focus is to prepare your timetable in the form of a graph, with
vertical lines representing specific dates and parallel horizontal
lines indicating the time spans required for performance of each
separate task. This is the essence of the PERT (Program Evaluation and Review Technique) system so dear to industrial and
other managerial planners since it won fame some years ago by
guiding the complex development of the Polaris submarine mis-
sile system to completion ahead of schedule, thus significantly
changing the balance of world military power.

Once you've worked back from all the mandatory dates

within the anticipated life span of your project, made allowance for holidays and local events and other dates which might affect your plans, and plotted the necessary interrelationships between various work segments of your plan, you should reexamine your timetable in view of two special possibilities for improving the quality of a volunteer performance.

First, you should divide the entire project into distinct major phases. This is important not only for coordination, but because it provides diplomatic occasions for reassigning your available manpower. You'll inevitably discover that some of the people to whom you've delegated vital responsibilities are incompetent, unable to get along with others, undependable, or procrastinators who disrupt your schedule. Their egos may prevent their recognizing their own inabilities and stepping aside. Diplomacy and politics and personal feelings may prevent you from insisting that they do so; firing a volunteer is a tough task. Furthermore, later recruits may demonstrate capabilities which should be used in top assignments. A divided phase timetable provides you with specific opportunities for shuffling leadership and specialized assignments for the most effective possible use of the manpower at your disposal.

Secondly, you should incorporate into the timetable certain progress checkpoints, so that everyone will know when particular jobs are to be completed. This provides a published, easily accepted excuse for various levels of leadership to check on the accomplishments of those working under them ("Since we've got to complete this door-to-door canvass in three days, I'm calling to find out how many houses each canvasser covered in this first day —to see whether we're in trouble or not"). Because it's so hard to fire volunteers (and you need their help!), the best way to discipline them is by obtaining progress reports related to a known timetable.

The second document you'll want as part of the end product of advance planning is an organization chart (see Appendix IV). If the plan has already been expressed in terms of a timetable, this is simply a matter of restating each task in terms of people rather than time. As you move from phase to phase, the same people can be reused for additional tasks, but you should be more concerned with how many people you can use than with how few you've absolutely got to have.

Think in terms of three aspects of organization: decision-making, special talents or experience, and mass manpower.

There should be a clear-cut chain of command throughout the organization, so that everyone knows where to turn for instructions, information, and policy decisions regarding unforeseen problems or opportunities. The basic decision-making body (generally the full membership convened in a formal meeting) belongs at the top. Right beneath that will come an executive body (similar to your steering committee) which is authorized to make all but the most basic decisions—within specified limits—in behalf of the full membership, without convening a meeting. Beneath that small group will come the chairman or president of the organization (you, assuming you're accorded this role by the initial organizational meeting). Then will come the unit leaders of each major aspect of the program.

In the case of a political campaign, such democratic niceties as a full-membership assembly which has ultimate authority and an executive committee which makes interim decisions in its behalf are normally done away with. The leader is the candidate, and at the risk of losing occasional supporters by the choices he or she makes, this candidate is the ultimate decision maker. Nevertheless, a candidate will want to establish a chain of command indicating other people who will make decisions of secondary importance within their particular areas of operation.

The decision-making chain of command is normally also the basic communication channel for the organization. Information can be spread rapidly down the pyramid if each person relays it in chain reaction form to everyone beneath him in the organization chart.

And, unless you have sufficient manpower from the very beginning, the decision-making chain is also the recruiting structure. The executive committee or the chairman recruits and assigns the key function leaders; each of these recruits his own assistants; each assistant recruits the workers needed to carry out his assigned task.

The organization chart should be constructed so that no one individual is supervising or maintaining communication with or recruiting more than a reasonable number of subordinate workers. Depending on the time available for the project and the complexity of the tasks, the span of control—the number of others for whom any supervisor at any level is responsible—might vary from two to ten. The smaller this span of control throughout your entire organization chart, the more likely you are to function smoothly, maintain good control, keep to your schedule, and get the results you need.

The second element of your organization chart—after the chain of command has been depicted—is specialization: particular talents, areas of experience, or other functions which support the major campaigning apparatus without cluttering up that chain of command. Someone should be in charge of publicity and have an adequate team of supporting recruits. Quite possibly you'll want a continuing research section—less extensive but more variously utilized than your preorganization research team —to keep up with what the opposition is doing, to make analyses of changes in public opinion, to keep you informed of new information supplementing the background research report. Someone should be in charge of central administrative functions— keeping records, maintaining files, handling correspondence. Finances should be separated from general administration, so that whoever keeps the books and maintains the bank account can function exclusively as a guardian of the public (and membership) trust, rather than an agent of the operational leadership.

If your project will require extensive financing, fund raising may become part of the mass appeal campaign. (Like recruiting, fund raising is a good device for getting a lot of people involved, and thus cultivating their continued support.) If considerable fund raising is required, but you believe it can be accomplished without mass appeals (and decide that this is more desirable), you'll want to establish fund raising as a specialized function separate from financial accounting, since the personality types who'll be best at these two functions are somewhat different. (See Chapter Twelve.) If very little money is needed, such simple expedients as modest membership dues or collections at meetings may be all the fund-raising machinery you need, and your normal finance section can handle that.

Among the specialists, you may also want to recruit professional or technical people who will lend their expertise to the project by advising its leadership. An attorney is likely to be especially valuable in this respect.

Remember that these specialists are going to be working largely behind the scenes, supporting the mass appeal campaign, but not significantly broadening the ground it can cover. Consequently, they should be placed in the organization chart in such a way that does not interject them between levels of operational decision making. And since some of their talents will be quite rare—and will have a qualitative impact on the entire scope of your project—you should get the most possible mileage out of the best people you can recruit and keep the number to a minimum.

In the third element of organization—the utilization of mass manpower—the very opposite guideline should be used: plan your organization to use as many people as possible on simple, limited commitment, bottom rung tasks. Again we return to that principle that the greater the number of people you involve in the campaign itself, the greater its chances of having broad public impact. Each additional recruit multiplies geometrically into a number of additional supporters on election day, or petition day, or whenever general public opinion comes into play.

For this reason, as well as for the added impact of face-to-face communication, you should be prejudiced in favor of door-to-door literature distribution rather than mailings. When you do turn to mass mailings, break the workload (addressing and stuffing envelopes, preparing lists, etc.) into small segments that will provide assignments for as many people as possible. For door-to-door distributions, surveying, petition signature canvassing, etc., think in terms of the smallest feasible number of households for each canvasser and the greatest possible number of canvassers. Consider mass telephoning operations as another means of involving recruits. Don't overlook occasions on which a crowd is an asset; simply being part of your crowd—as a show of strength at a public meeting or a demonstration—can be the element of involvement which causes dozens of people to begin identifying your cause as their cause.

Don't wait to see how many people you're going to have; design the organization chart before organizing; concern yourself only with the top layer of people; recruiting the next echelon—which in turn will recruit the next, and so on down to the foot soldiers who ring doorbells and stuff envelopes and canvass by phone—will be their task. This process of recruitment will be one of the major factors in the success or failure of your project.

If it later develops that you have too few recruits to fill all the slots in your organizational chart, you can always double up on assignments. But even if you think you can man your whole project with a dozen people, you'd be foolhardy to pass up any opportunity to mobilize support by providing a role for anyone who can be persuaded to help.

The final two documents which complete the planning process are a budget (see Appendix V) and a set of by-laws (see Appendix VI). Generally, these should be prepared after the timetable and organizational chart have put solid flesh on the bones of your general plan.

The budget should be charted in much the same way as the timetable—by assigning a dollar cost to each specialized function and each campaign task or stage. Cast against these costs should be an estimate of the funds your program is designed to raise during each time segment. The basic plan is not complete until it has been amended so that anticipated funds cover anticipated costs in every phase. (And you'll be wise to estimate costs liberally and available funds conservatively; a well-staged operation which can't afford to go into its next phase will be as disruptive and demoralizing as a poorly planned one.)

The by-laws, finally, are merely the formal rules which legitimize all of these plans. Make them as simple as possible—a statement of the purpose for which, and terms on which, a group of people have agreed to work together, and the arrangements whereby individuals will be empowered to speak or act or make decisions in the name of the group. (Formal by-laws are obviously unnecessary for a political campaign.)

Do not allow by-laws to become detailed; this will so inhibit your operational leadership that no decisive response to fast-changing circumstances will be possible without the cumbersome device of a general membership meeting. You'll spend far too much time in meetings, and far too little working to influence the general public to do what you want it to do.

By-laws should stipulate conditions of membership. They should provide for dues if this is to be your basic fund-raising mechanism. They should contain conditions for their later amendment. They should identify only the top decision-making positions in the organization chart—the people directly empowered to act for the membership between meetings—but should allow those leaders to delegate authority to act to as many others as necessary.

Thus a timetable, an organization chart, a budget and a set of by-laws (each of which can be prepared in detail by a single delegated member of the steering committee, after guidance has been provided by your general discussions of objective and approach) describe the entire anticipated career of your project or organization. Now you're ready to see how many people will join you in initiating the enterprise (after giving them an opportunity to exercise democratic judgment and perhaps make some amendments).

This is the purpose of the organizational meeting. You have one more task before your steering committee is dismissed and that meeting convenes—preparing an agenda. But let us examine that in sharper perspective in the next chapter, by seeing what it should include as the meeting itself unfolds.

PART TWO

Campaigning

CHAPTER EIGHT

"Going public"—the organizational meeting

The vast majority of volunteer campaigns seeking public approval of some proposed community innovation never develop to any greater scope than the preorganizational activities which we've discussed in the preceding chapters. The fact that approximately half of this book is devoted to getting organized—before the general public is brought into the project—is not accidental.

Once you announce your plans to the community and begin campaigning openly, perhaps the greatest single factor determining success or failure will be *momentum*. Large numbers of people will withhold their commitment until they can estimate your prospects for achieving your goal. Visible evidence of prompt and steady progress will convince them of the feasibility of the venture and thus reduce their hesitation to join you. An inactive lull after your public announcement (such as would occur if you had not completed your basic research in advance, or involved enough preliminary recruits to keep things moving, or planned your tactics and timing so that new recruits can be put to work promptly) will be seen as evidence that you lack sufficient public support to stand a good chance of achieving your objective; then you'll find people very reluctant to associate their names with, and give their time to, what looks like a losing cause.

The progressive momentum you create will also have a decided effect upon those who oppose your venture. If you've been reasonably discreet about what you are planning, those whose power or property or prejudices are going to be negatively affected will have to wait until your first public meeting to begin planning their countermeasures. If you've done the work outlined in the previous chapters, you're two or three months ahead of them. Furthermore, you have a sound grasp of the situation which will enable you to respond quickly and soundly to each new development, whereas opponents working without such thorough preparation are very likely to make serious and obvious mistakes in their spontaneous reactions to new developments.

If you'll pardon a martial comparison, think of a military attack on a specific objective. Days, weeks, often months of planning have gone into the operation before the first shot is fired. Maps have been studied, the enemy has been scouted, the right combination of troops and equipment and supplies has been carefully maneuvered into position, without revealing any more than necessary to the enemy. All of this is done in preparation for a few hours of intense commitment. But if it has been done properly, one side advances smoothly, and gains that vital psychological edge which comes from the feeling of winning, while the other side progressively crumbles beneath the weight of surprise, disorganization, and a collapse of morale.

The public meeting at which you formally organize your project and invite the community to join in its fulfillment is the opening shot of your attack on the status quo. But, as the chapter arrangement of this book suggests, by the time you fire that shot you are in reality already halfway through the campaign. The advance work you have done enables you to capture the initiative at this point, hold that initiative by displaying impressive momentum, and maintain your perspective and your control amidst the competitive distractions of the campaign. In short, your ammunition is in order, and you are ready for action.

The timing of your organizational meeting may have been dictated by mandatory dates on your campaign calendar. It must be held sufficiently far in advance of an election day, a petition deadline, etc., to allow for the smooth unfolding of your plan. It must take into account preliminary deadlines. For instance, while you could officially file your candidacy for a public office on the legally required filing deadline without beginning the public organization of your campaign, there's no point to such a delay. Opponents now know what you plan to attempt, so unless you organize openly and show progress at this stage, you may lose that all-important initiative which could convince the voters you're the probable winner; people like to be with the winner.

But if there are no mandatory deadlines—if you're seeking to create public opinion pressures behind a proposal the City Council could act on at any time, or form a cooperative which can begin operating as soon as you raise a certain amount of money—the timing of your organizational meeting is essentially a dramatic question. Carry your quiet background preparations as far as they can usefully go without public support, publicity, and broad-base recruiting. Allow plenty of time between the organizational meeting and your target date for reaching your goal; remember that your recruits will be moving at the slow-motion pace of volunteer activities (to which few people will commit more than three or four hours a week). But do not allow too much time; the organizational meeting should be close enough to your anticipated project-completion date to make it possible for you to maintain momentum, displaying constant activity and progress, throughout the entire period of the public campaign.

We've already discussed the roles your advance planning, research, publicity, and attendance promotion will play in the success of the organizational meeting. The specific uses of your planning and research results within that meeting will be more clearly demonstrated as we chart the agenda of a typical meeting.

But it would be well to reiterate here the necessity for careful coordination of advance publicity and attendance-promotion activities before this meeting. As soon as your first advance publicity has demonstrated to the community that a significant problem or opportunity exists, you have created a community leadership vacuum. The public realizes that, at least potentially, something needs to be done—and nobody is doing it. The dramatic function of the organizational meeting is to step into that vacuum and seize quick control of whatever interest your revelation of the problem (or opportunity) has provoked.

The specific date, time, and place of the organizational meeting should, then, be made as widely known as possible. If you have created news by revealing a problem, your announcement of a potential solution (the organizational meeting) will be equally newsworthy, and news media will help you spread the word. If local media don't exist, or decline to publicize your plans for a meeting, there are other ways to spread the word (and they should be used *in addition* to media publicity even when you are getting good news coverage).

Every community has a variety of bulletin boards—in public offices, in schools, in churches, and other meeting spots, often in community-service-conscious stores or offices. How many of these you will be allowed to use may depend on the nature of your project; but remember, at this date you have proposed no solutions; you are merely calling a meeting to consider solutions. You're still somewhat noncontroversial. Your preliminary publicity coordinator can, with a few telephoning assistants, reenforce the impact of news media coverage by systematically investigating all of the community's bulletin board opportunities.

Sympathetic business proprietors may allow you to display posters in their show windows; their hesitation will be directly proportional to the controversy your proposal inspires. But again remember that at this stage you are only proposing a meeting, not a course of action.

A telephone canvass of the leaders of other community organizations may induce a number of them to announce your organizational meeting at their own meetings or in their newsletters. During this purposefully vague period when no one knows exactly what you have in mind, you'll find that even unsympathetic people will extend such minor courtesies to avoid the possibility of later accusations of uncivic prejudice.

In a small community, if your steering committee and your research team have involved a dozen or more people, you may be able either to divide up the phone book and directly contact each family about the organizational meeting or to mail invitations to every family, or even to combine mail and phone calls for double impact. (This is obviously the work of your meeting attendance coordinator, not your publicist.)

For even more intensive attendance promotion, given the manpower, you should consider such face-to-face devices as the opinion survey referred to earlier.

However ambitiously you pursue such across-the-board public appeals for participation, make a separate and even more concentrated effort to get people who've already indicated potential interest to attend the meeting. The objective of this secondary campaign should be to *insure* that, whatever turnout your general efforts create, there *will* be enough people at the meeting to impress the news media, demonstrate public support from a variety of quarters, and provide at least the minimum number of recruits necessary to establish momentum, carry out immediate tasks, and hold the initiative as opposition develops.

At this point, let's retreat into the earlier phases of your preparatory work and mention a simple technique which will stand any community leader, innovator, or organizer in good stead, time after time. This is a card file of individuals interested in any phase of community life which particularly concerns you.

Whenever people speak up at public hearings, civic organization meetings, or even informal discussions of community problems, make notes of those who exhibit special concern or knowledge about problems which interest you. When you organize your steering committee, urge all members to make similar notes of people who display any evidence of potential concern about the problem you are going to attack.

Review newspaper files and organizational records covering past projects somewhat related to the one you are about to launch. Check the names of people who worked in those campaigns against the phone book, and list all who are still in the community.

As you recruit steering committee members, researchers, and other preorganizational volunteers, make notes on everyone you talk to who refuses for some reason which may be temporary (such as another immediate commitment); perhaps their situation will change before your organizational meeting. As your researchers interview public officials, local professionals, and others, insist that they add to your list everyone whose responses indicate possible sympathy.

Check the lists of officers of other organizations whose nature is somehow related to your project. Compare notes in the steering committee on the people with whom all of you have worked in prior projects or organizations.

Whether this name-collecting process has been a long-time habit with you, or was begun only with the establishment of your steering committee and preparations for this specific project, during your preliminary research and planning period you should be able to compile a considerable list of potential participants in your organizational meeting. If you have conducted a broad-based survey as part of your preorganizational build-up, the questionnaires and door-to-door interviews will have identified many additions to the list.

Your attendance-promotion coordinator should see that every person on this list gets a written invitation to the organizational meeting at the first point at which it is announced to the public—spelling out the purpose, the time, and the place. And each of these people should be followed up by telephone, or by a personal visit from one of your partisans.

In these follow-ups, try to get the individual committed. Don't just invite them and wait until meeting night for their response; ask: "Can you be there?" Call back again to those who are uncertain. And in every instance, stress the importance of attendance at this critical stage. (Remember, they only have to agree that an important problem or opportunity exists; since you haven't announced any specific plan, you aren't asking them to commit themselves to anything more than attendance at a meeting to consider what can be done.)

Use the telephone or postal cards to give those on your list a last-minute reminder a day or two before the meeting. This not only jogs memories; it underscores the mild obligation they've assumed in responding positively to the invitation by showing them that others are counting on them.

Make a point of inviting some people who will not be expected to join the cause—but whose presence will help create the impression of wide interest, and who may help spread the word about your project. All appropriate members of the press should be invited; phone the news desks of large metropolitan media and ask for the names of their community correspondents, or the specialists who cover your area of concern, so that your invitations to these reporters can be personal and specific. Invite observers from other organizations and public officials who may lend constructive observations even though they shy from firm commitments. Don't overlook the clergy, most of whom have a strong desire to keep abreast of developments affecting the community's style of life whether they become directly involved or not.

Despite all these efforts, you should have a contingency plan as to what you will do if bad weather, last-minute competing developments, or other causes prevent good attendance at your meeting. And quite frankly, the best contingency plan is a resolution to go ahead anyhow; announcing a postponement or a rescheduling is, in effect, announcing a failure in your first public effort—a sure way to destroy momentum and undermine public confidence in your prospects.

So get firm assurances from your steering committee, researchers, and other preorganizational recruits, and perhaps a few friends on whom you know you can depend, to make certain that at least a dozen people will turn out come hell or high water. Be prepared to go through the motions of organizing with only this small group, if necessary. If the public has shown so little interest, the press probably has too, and may well not have covered the meeting in person. Your news release immediately after the meeting may thus be able to stress progress without revealing the lack of public attendance.

But that's the worst of all possible cases; if you've done a reasonable job of preparing for the meeting, you should not have to be ashamed of the attendance figures (whether or not you get the publicity bonus of an overflow crowd).

Now comes the big moment. Meeting time arrives, and you as chairman of the steering committee bang the gavel or call for attention, as the host. You have in hand your agenda—the point-by-point schedule of topics the meeting will cover. Although the agenda must be prepared in advance, we have declined detailed discussion in the previous chapters because the clearest way to demonstrate what must be prepared is to imagine the meeting itself.

The term "organizational meeting" can be misleading. Actually, if you have followed the preliminary steps outlined in the first half of this book, you've already organized the project. The purpose of the organizational meeting is to legitimize your plans—to place behind them the force of every member of the community who is willing to join you, to enable you to speak in the name of a significant public, rather than a small private group.

In a sense, then, the organizational meeting could become a contest between democracy and leadership control. What if the people who attend your meeting accept your objectives—and agree to become an organization committed to achieving those objectives—but reject the specific plan you and your steering committee have so carefully prepared?

First, let it be said that such a development is highly unlikely. As your plans are presented to the meeting, the research and thought already devoted to the project will be obvious. People who are just being introduced to the subject will be far less secure in their spontaneous ideas and suggestions than the members of your steering committee and other preliminary recruits—the people who've shaped your plan. Even when they do make suggestions which conflict with your plans, they can be easily dissuaded by the weight of evidence and forethought which your core recruits can bring to bear.

But accept the possibility that some of these spontaneous suggestions may be good ones. Also remember that when you use the machinery of democratic procedure to gain the right to speak in behalf of a large public, you acquire an obligation to let that public make the ultimate decisions. With the deck so well stacked by your preliminary work, you can afford to be flexible, tolerant, patient.

Leave it to the other members of the steering committee to present the proposals of the preorganization group and defend those proposals, steering them toward eventual acceptance by the organizational meeting with only such alterations as do not cripple the over-all program. As chairman, you must maintain a studied neutrality which convinces the newcomers that they've had an opportunity to reshape advance plans, whether they've used that opportunity or not. (This is more than a moral obligation; pushing through a prepared plan with little opportunity for discussion and amendment will convince at least part of your new audience that it is being railroaded; most casually interested people will respond to such a conviction by simply declining to become involved, thus defeating the purpose of your organizational meeting.)

There is, of course, the possibility that people who are strongly opposed to any public action in the area indicated by your advance publicity will have suspected your purposes and will attend the meeting with plans to disrupt it. But again, you as the chairman must remain neutral.

Cope with these negative possibilities by preparing your steering committee. At their last meeting before the formal organizing session, you might play the "What if?" game once more. Let the group suggest the most likely possibilities of disruption and discuss generally how they as individual participants in the meeting could respond to each. This should focus their thoughts sufficiently to enable them to handle any such contingency which arises.

Remember that in cases of deliberate disruption by people who obviously want to see your project fail, your steering group is entitled to a certain ruthlessness—sometimes a necessary part of their commitment to see the project through to success. Urge them in advance to take the floor and identify known disrupters to the others present, pointing out the property or political interests which are motivating those disrupters. Advise them to ask questions of unknown disrupters in an effort to reveal true motives to the group. Once an individual can be shown to have a strong, selfish vested interest, an audience can be counted on to ignore that individual.

But so much for defensive precautions. Generally speaking, your steering group's focus will be positive. They have come well prepared to get a certain result from the meeting: the creation of a formal organization, adoption of your general plan by that organization, probably endorsement of your preliminary leadership as the leadership of the new organization, and the delegation of assignments which will involve the new manpower generated by the meeting in the inner workings of what has so far been a more or less private group. Your agenda should be arranged to accomplish all of this.

No one, specific agenda outline will cover all the requirements of all such newly formed ventures. But the one which follows covers all of the ground which must generally be covered and, with variations, should provide suitable guidelines for planning any organizational meeting. So here we go:

(1) *You call the meeting to order as its host.* You'll probably want to wait a few minutes after the announced meeting time if latecomers are still arriving, because in a large group repetition is not as feasible as it was in the smaller circle of your steering committee.

While you're waiting, start circulating a sheet of paper on which participants can list their names and phone numbers. This list will, hopefully, multiply your pool of known manpower.

But don't wait so long that early arrivers grow restless. Certainly ten minutes is the most you owe a public which has been so well prepared. In fact, if it's feasible, starting exactly on time will quickly create that impression of momentum and progress and decisiveness which is so important to morale and initiative.

(2) *State clearly but briefly the purpose of the meeting.* One sentence about the community problem or opportunity which motivated those who called the meeting is all you need; leave it to your steering committee and research-team members, in subsequent background information reports, to prove the case. But focus everyone's thoughts by pointing out that the purpose of the meeting is *not* to solve the problem, but to establish an organization which can solve it.

(3) *Legitimize the proceedings by calling for the election of a temporary chairman (to preside) and clerk (to keep minutes).* While it is almost inevitable that the group will quickly nominate you to preside, don't leave this to chance. At your final steering committee meeting, make sure that one member has been clearly designated to make this nomination immediately. (This is not an ego exercise; the steering committee wants to maintain control in order to get its plan adopted, and the clearest way to do this is to see that its chairman chairs tne organizational meeting. It is highly unlikely that a newly assembled group will offer any opposition to such an obvious nomination.)

But you can make good use of the temporary position of

clerk to broaden the sense of involvement of the newcomers. In reviewing the agenda at your final steering committee meeting, agree upon one member who can fill this position if necessary (and assign someone to make the nomination), but also agree that this nomination is to be withheld unless it is absolutely necessary. Then urge the entire steering committee to look over the arriving crowd for people who have not been part of your preparatory efforts, but who are known to have some popular support in the community or to represent segments of the community which could become valuable allies.

Urge your steering committee members to nominate two or three such newcomers for the temporary clerk's position as soon as you have been elected temporary chairman and have invited nominations for clerk. A mild, spontaneous contest at this early stage will underscore the enterprise's commitment to democracy.

These temporary offices should be dealt with quickly and casually; just invite nominations and call for a show of hands—without speeches by the nominees; these temporary officers will be replaced later in the meeting, so no one will resent quick decisions. The whole process of calling the meeting to order, stating its purpose, and electing a temporary chairman and clerk should take no more than five to ten minutes, and such dispatch will assure the crowd that progress is going to be made in a prompt and orderly manner, thus establishing a tone of momentum and initiative which will be useful throughout the project.

(4) *State very clearly, but without defensive elaboration, that a number of private citizens have already investigated the problem or opportunity which is the basis for the meeting.* Point out that much time can be saved by sharing their information and thoughts with the entire group. Announce who they will be and what they will offer, while assuring the group that you will keep this limited-participation portion of the meeting to a minimum. For example:

"Several of the people here have been thinking about this problem for some time, and they've talked to some experts and collected a great deal of essential background information. I'm

going to ask Bill Jones to tell you, in three or four minutes, what they've concluded might best be done. Then Agnes Brown will fill you in quickly on the legal angles, and Martin Green will give us an idea of how much money is involved, and Cindy Black will point out how much it could cost the community to let this problem go unsolved. Feel free to question all of them as they make their reports. Tom Smith has prepared a simple set of by-laws which would get us set up as an organization dedicated to doing something about the problem—but before we get to him, or to making any decisions, let's hear what Bill has to say."

(5) *Give the floor first to one member of your steering committee who is prepared to outline briefly the general course of action underlying your preliminary plans.* He shouldn't go into details; all that's needed is a simple statement of (a) the specific objective: "The best thing we could do to combat teen-age drug usage would be to see that a properly qualified youth officer—a trained social worker—is added to our police force" and (b) the approach: "The best way to get such an officer on the force is to collect a thousand signatures on a petition before the City Council completes its new budget, to show them the public demands this"—both of which were agreed upon by the steering committee.

No motion is in order at this time, because the meeting has not yet constituted itself as an organization prepared to follow any course of action. The only reason for outlining the proposed course of action this early in the meeting is to provide a mental peg to which people can attach the additional information they are about to receive. The research reports which follow will make the feasibility of the proposal obvious and thus increase the likelihood that your general plan will be adopted, without ruling out the possibility of amendments or other proposals.

(6) *Next, introduce members of your steering committee or research team for brief background reports on the most important aspects of the problem or project.* Instruct the first one on the agenda to refer to the availability of the background research report which has already been used in developing advance publicity, but do not circulate that report at this time (or at the

beginning of the meeting); otherwise people will be scanning the report instead of listening to your speakers.

Don't try to cover the whole research report. Hit only the most vital topics, with one person covering each topic in a very few minutes of summary presentation. Tell the meeting what it needs in order to decide whether or not it wants to tackle the project and to agree upon a general approach. Leave the details to be picked up and absorbed and utilized by appropriate people as they actually go to work on the operational tasks of the venture. Try to present the general approach and the background information in twenty to thirty minutes, including time for a few questions from the floor, so that people are ready to get involved in decision making (and thus, personal commitment) before they've become tired or bored or restless from being required to function primarily as listeners.

(7) *Now call on "Tom Smith" to present his proposed by-laws.* In this case, you should have sufficient copies available for distribution to everyone present. You might have Tom merely hit the high points while the audience is scanning its copies, since people will inevitably be half-listening and half-reading at this stage.

The steering committee member who presents these by-laws should, immediately upon concluding, turn to the chair and say: "Mister Chairman, I move that this group establish itself as a formal organization by adopting these by-laws, with the provision that every person who chooses to remain here be considered a member in good standing for the balance of this meeting, after which the stated conditions of membership will determine participation in future meetings." This provision is necessary to prevent the necessity of stopping the meeting to collect dues, sign a membership book, or otherwise authorize people to vote on subsequent motions. Furthermore, it has the psychological advantage of allowing everyone to get personally involved by operating as a member before they have to take any deliberate, individual step to become one.

Another member of the steering committee should be primed to offer a quick second to the by-law adoption motion.

(8) *The minute you hear this seconding motion, inter-*

rupt from the chair to remind the group that its proceedings are now "for real." You're saving a week or two by adopting ready-made by-laws rather than appointing someone to draft a set for a later meeting. Unless they suspect they are being railroaded, almost any group will welcome this opportunity for quick progress (and fewer meetings), but you must allay any such suspicions. Do so by pointing out that amendments from the floor are in order or that a substitute motion to delay action until another meeting will be acceptable to the chair. Have another steering committee member (preferably one who has not yet spoken) take the floor immediately and remind the group that under any circumstances by-laws would have to be drafted off the floor by some delegated individual or committee, and that nothing would be gained by delaying. That logic is very unlikely to be challenged.

At this point you might also assure the group of parliamentary democracy by stating that you will handle any subsequent motions or debate in the manner which seems fairest to you, but inviting any participant to challenge the rulings of the chair at any time, subject to an immediate majority decision to either support or overrule the chair.

(9) *Now ask for amendments or discussion of the by-laws.* Your steering committee, by prior agreement, should not enter this discussion until and unless it seems obvious that someone is about to put through an amendment, or a delaying motion, which would significantly conflict with your plan of action. Don't suggest opposition by reacting to it before it develops. But make sure the steering committee is prepared to tackle any opposition which arises and to push the by-laws toward acceptance after a minimum of noncrippling amendment. The worst thing that could happen to you would be to have the project sidetracked for a week or two at this stage by a delay in the formal establishment of the organization.

Following this pattern under normal circumstances, you can have converted your semi-private preliminary group into a duly constituted public organization in not more than an hour and translated your personal objectives into a genuine community concern.

(10) *Immediately upon adoption of the by-laws, refer to the section which establishes the post of chairman or president of the permanent organization and ask for nominations to this post.*

Often preliminary planners establish a nominating committee to present a slate of officers to an organizing meeting. But this is an unnecessary formality which may cause resentment by creating the impression that the meeting is being railroaded—an impression with which you've already flirted by such a display of advance planning and which you should offset in every way possible.

The steering committee should have already done the work of a nominating committee, by agreeing in advance to which of the formally created posts should be held by members of the advance preparation group and which can safely be left to newcomers (in the same manner and for the same reasons the temporary clerk's post was left open for new participants). The committee should have agreed on its candidates for each post it wishes to control and agreed upon back-up candidates for the other posts in case suitable nominations from the floor are not forthcoming.

Then, as you call for nominations, different members of your preliminary group should quickly nominate those choices and support them if opposition develops. Since your steering committee has never been identified as a group, these will appear as spontaneous floor nominations and arouse much less resentment than a nominating committee report might.

If this sounds too Machiavellian for your tastes, simply remember that your primary commitment is to an objective which will be in the public interest; ends don't always justify means, but neither does democracy require that you invite or encourage or make easy any opposition that will disrupt or severely compromise your pursuit of a worthy objective.

(11) *As the most visible leader present, it is very likely that you will be promoted from temporary to permanent leadership by the group; on being nominated, your next step is to yield the chair to the temporary clerk—another democratic nicety which will allay suspicions; do not preside over your own election.* Your

steering committee should be prepared for any unforeseen opposition and should make the most of the fact that you are obviously well prepared for the task. Once you're elected, proceed with the selection of other officers specified in the by-laws.

(12) *After these elections, return to the matter of the general plan outlined at the beginning of the meeting.* Invite the individual who presented that plan to move its adoption as a general course of action, under the direction of the elected officers. Discuss the plan, plus amendments or alternatives from the floor, under normal parliamentary procedure. Do not let the meeting drift toward adjournment until it has authorized its elected leaders to proceed immediately on a definite (though not overly detailed) plan of action, because your next task is going to be public evidence of progress and momentum, and that requires action.

(13) *Next, invite a motion to authorize such expenditures as will be necessary before the next anticipated general membership meeting.* You should be very meticulous about the formalities of spending the group's money; criticism in this area can hand your opposition an easily exploitable bonanza. Unless dues specified by the by-laws are to be your basic source of funds, this motion should also include authorization for necessary fund-raising solicitations in the name of the group.

Budgetary and fund-raising details should be left to the duly elected officers, particularly an executive board (which includes specific officers, and may also include members-at-large) empowered to act in behalf of the general membership between meetings (replacing your earlier steering committee). Details of the operational plan should also be left to the leadership. But the formalities of authorizing that leadership to act in the name of the organization should always be observed.

(14) *For obvious and immediate tasks implied by the adopted plan, either delegate responsibility to willing members right there at the organizational meeting or announce that you will make such assignments personally in the near future.* If you know your personnel well enough, it's best to do it on the spot, so all members will know who to contact about areas of activity which most interest them and will know that people who subse-

quently ask them to undertake secondary responsibilities are doing so as properly delegated leaders.

(15) *As the meeting draws to a close, summarize briefly your own impression of what has happened.* Often different people can reach different conclusions about the outcome of the same discussion. Eliminate ambiguities by summarizing whenever you consider it useful during a meeting—and always at the end of the meeting. Send everyone home with the same concept of what has happened and what will happen next.

(16) *Never adjourn without establishing agreement regarding the next meeting.* If your plans are straightforward, frequent or regular meetings may not be necessary; it's better to spend your time campaigning with the general public than to use it talking with each other. But unless a specific time and place for the next meeting can (and should) be announced at once, at least make sure that everyone knows *how* another meeting can be requested and for what purposes.

(17) *Invite a motion to adjourn.* Don't let the meeting drag; you'll keep alive that impression of momentum by adjourning with dispatch, as soon as the night's work is done. Those who want to explore this new idea you've introduced into their lives through rambling conversation can do so after adjournment—and you should be prepared to remain and give them that opportunity —but you'll preserve the commitment of those who don't by letting them get home or about their business as soon as possible.

No meeting of this sort should last over two hours; note target times beside each item on the agenda and prod the discussion away from digressions whenever this timetable is threatened.

One last service should be wrested from your preorganizational steering committee before they cease to function. Have the advance publicity coordinator on tap to deliver one more news release to all local media immediately after the meeting. This should be a release describing what happened at that meeting, in the most dramatic form possible, to display your momentum to an even broader public.

With that, you're in business.

Obviously if the approach you've chosen is that of a political candidacy, the format of the campaign-organizing meeting will be somewhat different from the 17-step agenda outlined in this chapter. Votes will be unnecessary, as will by-laws (unless a legally constituted campaign committee is required for handling of funds). But the general pattern of presenting a problem or opportunity, putting forth your candidacy as a specific means of dealing with that problem or seizing that opportunity, informing those whose interest you've attracted of the background facts which make your plan feasible, enlisting their personal involvement by drawing them into the discussion, and wrapping up the loose ends of who does what next is as applicable to a political campaign as it is to a public opinion campaign or a cooperative venture.

In either case, as a leader it is now your task to expand the bridgehead you've established and get the greatest possible number of people to work carrying out your plans as effectively as possible.

Let us turn, then, from plans to people.

CHAPTER NINE

Recruiting and assigning members

Only a small portion of any population is likely to work directly in efforts to change the status quo. In a normal community, something like 15 per cent of the people have enough grasp of how things work and enough confidence in themselves to play an active role in shaping community decisions. Only a small portion of these can be interested in any given project at any given time.

And since these "natural activists" tend to be already involved in other things, many of them have acquired interests in and obligations toward existing power arrangements which make them reluctant to "rock the boat"—or have future political aspirations which make them cautious about controversial commitments.

The moment your plans become public—through an organizational meeting, for instance—those whose property or power or prestige or plans are likely to be negatively affected by your venture can be expected to begin focusing opposition. Except in political campaigns, where the obvious way to beat one candidate is by putting up another candidate, this opposition may never be formally organized. It will, instead, take the form of individual or existing-group efforts to dissuade people from joining you.

Before lines of conflict solidify, there will be a brief and fluid period during which many of the community's potential activists could go either way—into your camp or into the opposition. Unless they have a strong and direct interest, their decisions are likely to be based on fairly superficial considerations, particularly on who talks to them first.

Immediately following your organizational meeting, then, you should be prepared for a fast and comprehensive effort to preempt the allegiances of these activists. This may involve leaving a number of top-ranking assignments vacant, since some of these people will be leaders more attracted by challenging roles than by simple tasks.

Immediately following your organizational meeting, call together the elected leaders and any people you have appointed to key roles and make a quick assessment of the audience that first meeting produced. Don't wait for such technicalities as dues paying or membership-roster signing. Go over the attendance list which you circulated during the meeting. Review the card file of potential supporters you built up prior to the meeting. But even more importantly, discuss the acquaintances of every member of your leadership group which has now, perhaps, been expanded by the organizational meeting elections.

Divide the names of possible recruits among this leadership group and start telephoning immediately. Examine the organization chart to pick specific first-phase assignments for each potential recruit (having an alternative or two ready in case the job doesn't interest a particular person). It's much easier to get people to agree to do a specific job than it is to win their total commitment to your project on vague terms which make it difficult for them to assess the time required or the soundness of your planning.

Then phone, phone, phone, as rapidly as possible. Make sure any who are personal friends of members of your leadership group are assigned to those members for recruitment. Don't be discouraged by those who turn you down; for every new volunteer you recruit, you'll also succeed in neutralizing several other people who won't help you, but have been sufficiently informed (and flattered) to dissuade them from joining any future opposition.

The real key to success, however, lies in breaking outside the limited circle of natural community activists and making activists of people who have never done this kind of thing before. Such people are likely to be more openminded—and more willing to do the grass roots leg-work of personalized campaigning—than are people who already enjoy some measure of community leadership.

There are two keys to such broad-base recruiting: simple, specific job descriptions and pyramided organization.

If at all feasible, your campaign plan should include a short phase immediately following the organizational meeting in which a large number of people can be used to do a very simple task. Door-to-door literature distribution, or a door-to-door or telephone survey asking straightforward questions (unless you've already done this to promote initial meeting attendance) is ideal. Confine the preparation of materials to a small group—preferably from your already educated (but no longer functioning) preliminary steering committee or research team—so that it can be done rapidly.

Establish a geographic division of the community on an actual map, such as those generally available at town or city halls, to keep everything concrete and specific. Assign your newer leaders the task of recruiting manpower, while the more indoctrinated group is preparing literature or survey materials.

Establish a well-defined pyramid, with a top-echelon leader in general charge of recruitment. Then divide the community into the smallest feasible number of subregions (remember that span of control) and appoint recruiting coordinators for each subregion. Redivide the regions into smaller units until you've gone down to the neighborhood and then the block level. Then start recruiting at the top, with each recruit being immediately assigned to enlist additional people for the next echelon.

Generally speaking, the recruiting pyramid should also be the supervisory chain of command for this first phase of operations. But some flexibility should be maintained, to allow very successful recruiters to help fill the charts of less effective ones. There is no reason why people need necessarily be confined to working in their own neighborhoods, but some attempt should be made to preserve geographic lines in recruiting, simply to force recruitment into all segments of the community.

Whatever this first phase of operations is, it should be simple and quick. During this phase you are going to learn a lot about a lot of new people. You'll want to incorporate into your plans a very early phase-change at which most assignments become obsolete, to give you an opportunity to shuffle people to take advantage of newly discovered talents and remove incompetents from the active chain of command.

In addition to your geographic assignments, you can make use of a number of additional people (perhaps your best ones) by creating a floating manpower reserve—one or more teams which can move quickly into areas where recruiting has not been successful or where poor supervision has hindered performance. Such a floating manpower pool is also a good device for testing those promising recruits who complete their geographic assignments early, by giving them a chance to serve as troubleshooters.

Keep everything as simple and informal as possible, but don't overlook the possibilities of improving performances through simple training procedures. Clear-cut instruction sheets should be available to each echelon of recruits, to guard against misinterpretation or faulty communication as recruitment and explanation and supervision move down the pyramid. Demonstrations (in the form of simple skits) can reassure the hesitant that there's really no more to the task than you've said there is.

Making sure that everyone has basic information about the organization and timing of the project is an absolute necessity. Subordinate leadership echelons will be hesitant to push volunteers for prompt performance; but a published timetable provides an easily accepted motive for doing so; the subordinate leader is able to appeal to the timetable to demonstrate that he, too, is under pressure, that his prodding is designed to keep his part of the program from delaying others, rather than merely to exercise his authority.

A subtle form of training can be accomplished without presumption—without making extra time-demands—by pairing volunteers into two-member teams. Working alone, an individual may take too many short cuts—for example, by using the phone when he's been assigned to make face-to-face contacts. Two individuals working together will be less likely to expose such negligence to each other, and as they observe each other, they will learn new techniques and establish confidence in old, obvious ones. If your communications and control are good enough, you can get extra mileage out of this pairing technique by constantly changing the pairs, particularly by splitting each team after each round of work and giving each individual a new recruit to "break in" the next time out.

There is really very little to ringing a doorbell, or dialing a telephone, and asking a prepared question or communicating specific information or requesting a signature on a petition form. But it is surprisingly difficult to get a lot of people to do it systematically on a community-wide scale. Thus the need for a clearly understood, pyramided structure with short spans of control (each person responsible for only a small number of other people), unambiguous instructions, definite time deadlines, and such training and orientation arrangements as seem useful.

Even on this simple basis, you'll run into personality problems which upset your plans. Most of them will take two forms—personality clashes and pure nonperformance.

An abrasive personality in a volunteer organization is just as likely to cripple performances higher up in the organization chart as it is to discourage enthusiastic performance on lower echelons. Amateur leaders will be reluctant to make repetitive contact with unpleasant workers whose efforts they are supposed to supervise. Communication and time discipline break down.

In many cases a personality clash is not generated by unreasonable behavior by either party; it simply stems from incompatibility; one person's normal tone of voice seems gruff and disapproving to another person, who may be slightly sensitive to criticism or rebuff.

You'll have neither the time nor the diplomatic leeway to examine every interpersonal relationship within the organization to prevent all such barriers to communication and supervision. But if you'll ask for detailed reports at regular intervals, the problems will become apparent. Where supervisors *know* no progress has been made, you simply have a nonperformer on your hands. Where supervisors *don't know* whether progress has been made or not, it is quite possible that you have a personality clash which is impeding communication.

Nonperformers can be substituted for by those "floating reserves" we mentioned earlier, as long as each echelon keeps checking progress often enough and thoroughly enough to spot the gaps. Reshuffling of assignments at the end of each phase of the project will enable you to remove such nonperformers from essential functions. In many cases they'll quietly drop out of your project, so relieved that they've been allowed to go gracefully that their eventual partisanship will not be affected.

But if a nonperformer (or an eager incompetent, who works but doesn't get results) fails to fade away in the next phase or is so severely disrupting coordinated operations that you can't wait for a phase change to replace him, resort to what we might call the "old elephant" technique. You've read how old elephants wander away from the herd to die in privacy. Give your non-performing volunteer an independent task—one which could conceivably aid the project but is not essential and will not disrupt anything if it is never completed. Don't embarrass the volunteer by checking progress; let him wander off into the brush like an old elephant, unembarrassed by the periodic necessity to admit failures, but still a member of your team for as long as he wishes the identification.

Personality clashes between responsible, capable, committed people are more difficult to resolve. Under the casual circumstances of a volunteer project, it will probably be inappropriate for you to attempt to intercede to smooth out such clashes by bringing the parties involved to a better understanding of each other, even if you feel you have the capability to do so.

So your best advice is to separate the parties concerned. Remember that your organization chart includes a number of specialized functions not involved in the basic chain of command —administrative tasks, publicity, and research. By "promoting" one of the problem parties to headquarters to work in one of these specialized roles, you can reopen your lines of communication without offending anyone.

A certain amount of self-selection of future assignments will help eliminate such personality clashes after the first phase of operations. Be sure the entire organization receives adequate information about the organizational structure and the work to be done in subsequent phases. Invite people to indicate which type of activity they'd prefer (though not how far up the chain of command they'd like to work; top leadership should make those decisions on the basis of performance). With such options, people tend to regroup themselves into more congenial, smoothly performing units as the project evolves.

One of the major difficulties in volunteer organizations is the reluctance many of us feel about exposing ourselves to others. We are an incredibly bashful species. We don't like personal hostility, and we tend to avoid situations which might subject us to hostile reactions, from friends or strangers.

The more controversial your project is, the more crucial this innate sensitivity becomes; some people shrink from merely being refused when they ask for a work commitment, a vote, a signature, an opinion, or a dollar. But almost all of us shrink from being counterattacked by strangers who tell us how irresponsible or dangerous or radical we are because of our association with a given cause.

Yet exposure to the rough-and-tumble reactions of the public brings with it one of the most gratifying personal rewards of civic activism; we learn that hostility can't hurt us; we compare notes within the comradeship of the project, and such rebuffs become honorable wounds rather than humiliations. We emerge from such experiences more self-confident, more willing to make legitimate claims of life and society despite the intimidation of possible rebuffs.

This is a hard thing to explain to volunteers during recruiting conversations or training-orientation sessions. You don't want to alarm the hesitant by raising unpleasant prospects, and few of those who are particularly worried want to confess their sensitivity by asking for guidance.

Three techniques will be especially useful in coping with this widespread encumbrance to aggressive campaigning: (1) using yourself as an object lesson; (2) creating a deliberate "mythology" which enables you to talk about the problem; or (3) helping one echelon bring its personal inhibitions into focus by talking to it about the same problems on a lower echelon.

If you use yourself as an object lesson, a sense of humor will come in very handy. Whenever you suspect that personal sensitivity is preventing a key member of your organization from doing his job, find occasion to recall rebuffs which you have suffered, and kid yourself about them. The moment another person starts laughing with you, that person is well on the way to becoming able to keep public hostility in perspective, to accept a certain amount of it as inevitable and worth the risk.

By creating a deliberate mythology, we mean drawing your own characterizations of the opposition, wherever it appears, in a way which ridicules those who respond hostilely and subtly glorifies those who are willing to face such hostility. The civil rights movement, the Black Power movement, the student antiwar protest movement have carried this technique to a high level of sophistication, by making jail sentences badges of honor. This is a bit extreme for most community innovation campaigns, but it demonstrates how any movement can embolden its workers by creating its own standards of honor, often by creating its own definitions of opposing dishonor.

The third technique—bolstering one echelon by talking through it to another—has particular force in that it requires people to come to grips with their own weaknesses by committing themselves to combat those weaknesses in others. If you're worried about your neighborhood leaders committing themselves forcefully in the face of some inevitable hostility, talk to them about the problem as it affects their subordinate block leaders. For example:

"You'll find that a lot of your block leaders will get stalled the first time someone really talks back to them, and they'll be hesitant to ring the next doorbell. Or after two or three people turn them down by telephone, they'll procrastinate about calling the rest of their list. Such reactions are inevitable in a volunteer organization like ours. What can we do about it?"

After they've discussed the problem with you, they may never get around to applying suggested solutions to those working under them. But they will certainly have made some progress at bringing their own hesitancies and insecurities into focus.

In your first phase of activity, you'll have limited opportunity to choose carefully the people you assign to each slot in the organization chart. The necessity for maintaining control of a rapidly growing organization will dictate that you start at the top, filling slots with the first available people. The recruiting pyramid may well bring in much more capable people at lower echelons, but the politics of volunteer organization will make it difficult to demote early recruits in order to promote latecomers. Furthermore, you won't really know how competent most of your compatriots are until you've seen them in action.

But those same regular, frequent progress reports which are your disciplining device (because people will overcome procrastination when they know it will cause them the embarrassment of "no progress" confessions) will also identify your best performers. Sometimes poor performers will remove themselves from the chain of command to alleviate their own frustrations and newly identified result-getters can be shifted into their places. Whether or not this happens, the deliberately planned reshuffle necessitated by the transition into the next phase of the plan will enable you to make desirable adjustments diplomatically. This is why the first phase after the organization meeting should be a short one; don't penalize your project by allowing the random nature of original assignments to hold down good people too long.

You do not have to be an experienced executive to maneuver volunteers through such flexible, maximum utilization of human resources. You simply have to plan to do it this way and make certain that the phase changes and power-to-delegate which will make it possible are written into the timetable and the by-laws before the steering committee submits them to the organizational meeting.

Remember that the organization's leadership will undoubtedly continue to be dominated by those comrades who worked with you on the steering committee. They've helped set the stage for creative personnel management, and they understand why you have to maneuver people. Let them help you, by contributing their own performance observations and comparing notes on your assessments of the personalities and talents with which you are working.

CHAPTER TEN

The politics of membership

During the planning stages of your project, there were sound reasons for limiting your recruiting to people who knew each other and had worked together before. But now that you are campaigning in public, all of those reasons are obsolete.

And yet, because early recruiting has been on a very personal basis, it is highly likely that the core of your organization is drawn from a limited portion of the community. Not only does this leave you at a disadvantage in campaigning in other segments of the community; it can also create the impression that yours is a limited, special interest group. Furthermore, because you as a leader will learn most of what you need to know about public response to your proposals only from your own organization, this limited base of support will severely hamper your awareness of the community's attitudes toward your project.

It is very important, then, to take early and deliberate and insistent action to reach beyond your original recruiting successes, to reach into all areas of community opinion.

Under normal community project campaign circumstances, the best way to reach all segments of opinion is to build into your plan a deliberate and systematic program for attempting to expand your organization into all segments of the community. Recruiting conversations get right down to the bare essentials; when you honor people by asking them to join you, you're much more likely to get a sincere and substantive response than when you ask for distant consideration on election day or the often superficial act of signing a petition.

There are two general ways to spread your organization out from the closely knit group you needed for preliminary planning into a representative cross section of the community. One is geographic; you simply divide the community into map segments and cover them one by one. This requires a great deal of manpower—something you're not likely to have in the early stages when the character of your organization is becoming established.

The other is expansion through other organizations or similarly cohesive segments of the community which have their own lines of communication, their own special interests, their own hierarchies of recognized leaders—ethnic groups or distinctive, long-established neighborhoods, or such political subentities as wards and precincts.

Except in the case of a cooperative enterprise—where the essential goal is usually a certain amount of money to finance a new, semi-private service or institution and where the campaign need only extend as far as is necessary to raise that money, concentrating on the most likely prospective contributors—it is essential that any community improvement campaign be designed to reach, theoretically, the entire community. All will have a say in the eventual result, whether it be a demonstration of public opinion, or the casting of ballots; to deliberately ignore any segment of the community is simply to spot the opposition—or the forces of apathy—an unwarranted advantage. So your campaign should be designed to keep the pressure on the recruiting pyramid until your roster reaches into every neighborhood and cuts across all economic and religious and ethnic lines.

But this will be an end result and it won't come about from the natural recruiting directions of that small group of personal acquaintances from whom you developed a steering committee. The latter's backgrounds are probably similar; their combined familiarity with diverse segments of the community is probably confined to a narrow range.

It is important, then, that in all stages of recruiting, you exert deliberate pressure for expansion into new areas, new groups. You may have to break the ice yourself, by personally recruiting new people who can give you access to new elements of the population. You'll find it an exciting, eye-opening experience.

And as you recruit in new areas, you should make deliberate arrangements to draw a good cross section of these new people into the organization's leadership group. *Then* you'll know when you're likely to offend the Greeks, or what will inspire support from the labor unions, or what the young people think of your enterprise, because you'll have their representatives in your intimate discussions, trying as hard as you are to keep the campaign on the best track, win it new adherents, and save it from blunders.

Okay, so how do you do it?

If your community is of more than intimate size and of reasonably diverse character, you probably start well back in that preorganization stage. Once you've defined the problem or opportunity which is central to your endeavor, it is legitimate to seek a cross section of both leadership and lay opinion regarding it.

Use a special component of your research team to scout out all community organizations, all distinct ethnic and religious and neighborhood groupings, at a time when you can do it without making demands or implying commitments.

Start by listing every community organization, every church, every institution with a resident population which participates actively in community affairs, i.e., including schools and retirement homes, but excluding prisons or military installations which draw their population from beyond the community. List the civic clubs, and the political organizations, labor unions, local professional and business associations, veterans' organizations. You will generally find that distinct ethnic groups identify closely with a particular church—a good point of contact—but you may also discover ethnic social or political organizations. Where no organization provides precise contact with a given neighborhood, look for neighborhood improvement associations, the parent-teacher organization in the nearest school, or precinct political organizations.

Where do you get this information if it is not available in some previously published form? Two sources will give you a good start—the classified phone directory and the local newspaper. Sympathetic public officials who have traveled the political circuit before can be very helpful. But one of the very best sources for amplified information is clergymen; their members are often the leaders of local organizations and in many cases they are themselves real or honorary members of a dozen or more.

Of course, you'll need more than the names of organizations; you'll need the names of leaders with whom you can talk. The classified phone directory won't help here, but the newspaper and the politicians and the clergy can.

In fact, if no list of the community's organizations and their leaders is readily available, you'll find these same newsmen and politicians and clergymen eager to have one. You can eliminate all sorts of tensions and suspicions by designating the actual compilation of such a list, as a community service, as your essential purpose.

But you may need an organizational "front" to do this believably—one which has none of the partisan or controversial overtones of the project you are contemplating. Certainly some member of your steering committee is associated with some good cause which could use such a list for its regular public education or fund-raising campaigns—the United Fund, the Red Cross, the Boy Scouts. Have that member propose the compilation of such a list to such a noncontroversial organization and volunteer to compile it. Then provide your own manpower to help the volunteer keep that commitment, as well as a carbon copy of the list.

Generally, however, the compilation of the list will be much easier; your principal task will be in using it to spread your contacts into all segments of the community.

Scout the ground thoroughly before you inhibit people's responses by revealing the specific nature of your project. Take the same cautious approach suggested earlier for preliminary interviews with potentially defensive public officials.

Divide your list of community leaders among your available interviewers. Have them phone ahead and state simply that they are collecting ideas for coping with a community problem (identify the problem if necessary), and believe that because of the individual's role as a community leader, he or she might have some helpful thoughts. Don't take no for an answer, unless you can identify an alternate leader-contact in the same organization; if people insist that the subject isn't appropriate to their organizations, assure them that you're approaching them as individual community leaders, not as organizational spokesmen; if they contend that they know nothing about the subject, suggest that you want to share some interesting information, but that what you want from them is opinions about public reaction, not the technicalities of the problem; if they simply insist that they're not interested, remind them that their members may be and that this is an opportunity to do those members a service by seeing that those interests are expressed; if they persist in their refusal, urge them to suggest others from their group who might like to discuss the topic.

Don't overlook age groups as you explore the diversities of the community; if there are no organizations in the local high school or college even vaguely related to your central topic, interview student council or class officers; you'll probably find these young people flattered that some adult wants their opinions and is willing to listen for a change. Later they can be the key to an army of energetic manpower. And organizations consisting primarily of the elderly can give you contact with a segment of the community which is often left on the sidelines, but has a wealth of talent and experience—and sometimes money—to contribute.

In each interview, ask about other people who might be interested in the topic—who might have useful ideas. Don't confine suggestions to the same organization; this comprehensive approach to community leadership has already taken you out of your original in-group; now you can go as far as people's willingness to talk will take you.

Use the same graduated sequence of events in developing these contacts as we've suggested on other occasions; simply get to know people first, by asking their opinions in a noncommittal manner. Add those who display interest to your card file of potential recruits; ask those who don't to suggest others.

Then invite the promising ones to your organizational meeting; if they don't appear, make a deliberate attempt to recruit them shortly thereafter. Whenever appropriate, add them to your list of fund drive prospects. Put the important ones on your mailing list.

Your primary objective will be recruitment—to use these people as bridges to the varied segments of the community they represent. But there are also other opportunities. Later you may be able to persuade them to use speakers from your group in their regularly scheduled meeting programs. With some you may find enough interest to suggest their organization's formal endorsement of your cause or financial support. You can stimulate the flow of public communication by inviting observers from their organizations to your meetings.

If intense opposition arises, you may need some neutral forums for direct confrontations with opponents (if you think you'll gain more than the opponents will). The leaders of other organizations with which you have established contact by this systematic approach can provide such forums, without compromising their organizations.

The essential concern, however, is not how you use these contacts, but that you make them, and that you reactivate them from time to time. The inevitable broadening of your perspective will increase the impact of your public appeals and prevent that blind phenomenon of an organization talking primarily to itself.

For these reasons, your recruiting policy could well be one of the most significant aspects of your entire campaign; the politics of organizational membership is potentially a key to the politics of community acceptance.

CHAPTER ELEVEN

Publicity—why and how

Publicity—impersonal one-way communication to the general public through existing channels of communication or mass-produced statements—can reach far more people than the face-to-face efforts of your general campaign organization. But the impact is less intense, the conversions less binding, because no commitment has been exacted from your audience. Publicity, then, simply helps you improve the amount of eventual support you can expect when the indifferent and the uncommitted make superficial decisions—on election day, or when polls are taken—unless it is carefully planned and coordinated to serve other functions as well.

Publicity efforts which are timed to avoid any lulls of public attention can create that invaluable impression of momentum which prompts people to hurry aboard your bandwagon. Publicity which anticipates specific demands you are about to make on the community—for organizational meeting attendance, petition signatures, or what-not—prepares the ground for personal campaigning and makes it easier for your face-to-face solicitors to get what they want. Publicity which intersperses your most convincing arguments throughout legitimate reports of interesting news helps forestall opposition and neutralize converts the opposition might have won simply by getting there first. Publicity builds enthusiasm in—and actually helps you communicate with—your own organization.

A good publicity program walks a tightrope between legitimate journalism and self-serving promotion or psychological warfare. Your publicity team should assume a basically journalistic stance, as though their essential function was to keep the public fully informed about your activities, from the special vantage point of the insider.

Certainly your publicists are going to slant their reports

to the best advantage of your project. But in doing so, they must display a certain respect for public credibility; they should be prepared to admit occasional problems without undermining the impression of progress; they should be willing to acknowledge obvious odds and obstacles rather than undermining public confidence in what they say by demonstrating blindness to unfavorable facts.

But their first task will be the mechanics, not the tone, of publicity. What communications channels exist to give them access to the public ear and eye? What facilities must they have to take advantage of these opportunities? The most obvious, and generally most effective, channels are the news media which serve the community—local newspapers and radio stations, and metropolitan papers, radio stations, television broadcasters, and magazines.

A surprising number of community organizations never get beyond the most obvious possibilities. Where one local newspaper exists, they prepare their releases for that paper without taking the trouble to duplicate the same information for regional or nearby metropolitan media. Very little additional effort is required to send extra copies to these other media, but undue modesty causes them to forget that nonlocal media are often hungry for stories which will demonstrate their grass roots interest in the communities which make up their audience.

Frequently, too little attention is paid to the physical requirements of media. Radio stations may be far less interested in written reports than in tape-recorded statements which make it appear that they were on the spot. Television film clips are often expensive, but a few minutes in a commercial studio, filming a key announcement by you or one of your most prestigious associates, could be a good investment. Many newspapers will use photographs, and incorporate your basic message in the captions, far more readily than they use unsolicited publicity releases.

Radio stations frequently have telephone recording facilities as normal components of their news departments; asking about such facilities and offering to have organizational leaders rather than anonymous publicists prepare statements for this use may get better coverage. Offering to send spokesmen or exhibits to television studios, where they can be filmed without mobile equipment, will improve your chances. Making sure your photographs are of sufficient quality for good reproduction—clear focus, sharp contrasts, and clean enlargements—will greatly affect the prospect of their being used. Remember that print reproduction of photographs is generally improved when the original is larger than the reproduction; quality declines when the news medium must enlarge the original.

In larger news media, a number of people may be involved in the selection of material to be published or broadcast. When you prepare your basic distribution list for news releases (one of the first tasks your publicity team should complete), do not hesitate to include the names of several people from one important medium. A few extra postage stamps or sheets of mimeograph paper may multiply your chances of gaining public notice.

News media are generally commercial media, which depend on advertising for their ultimate goal, i.e., revenue. The relationship between publicity and advertising is a touchy one. With most reputable major news media, your news releases will be judged solely for their legitimate news value and used or discarded regardless of your willingness or unwillingness to buy advertising space or time.

But accept the fact that small local newspapers and radio stations are often monopolies and often so desperate for revenue that they do show favoritism toward advertisers. However much it pains you to do so, the investment of a few dollars in small ads or brief radio spots may, in addition to its direct communications impact, render the medium more susceptible to your unpaid publicity releases.

But don't confine your attention to the press. Your publicity team should take a prompt and systematic census of all bulletin boards and poster display opportunities within the community. Remember that the automobiles owned by your members are good display points, seen by many people in the course of a day. Local regulations on the posting of signs do not usually apply to cartop signs or bumper stickers.

Other organizations may provide communications channels which you can use. Are there those who would find it appropriate (and in their interests) to include your announcements in their own meetings, public services, ceremonies, or newsletters? The mail is, of course, a universal medium. The same equipment which you use to reproduce news releases can produce an informative newsletter, presenting your case to other community leaders as well as your own recruits at very little cost.

A comprehensive inventory of all such channels for mass communication will define the publicity team's work for it. The next step is to make available the equipment and the special talent which enable it to utilize these channels.

Too often, publicity processes are limited to whatever equipment and whatever talents are readily available. Expand your opportunities by deliberately seeking people who can take pictures, record sound, and draw posters, as well as those who can write.

Locate a mimeograph machine or spirit duplicator which can be used readily and regularly; find people with photographic darkrooms and recording equipment; access to photocopying equipment may be crucial when fast releases to several media are required to report the results of a meeting while it is still news. And of course, typewriters are essential. Make certain that necessary equipment will be available at odd hours; the older your news gets, the more likely the press is to ignore it; because most extracurricular organizations meet in the evening, the late night reproduction of news releases should be a regular feature of the publicity operation.

But these are only the minimum mechanical essentials. In the last analysis, news value will be the critical factor in determining how much exposure your publicity wins for your cause.

Remember that where controversy is involved, journalists are not without their share of the insecurities which affect the rest of us. Editors will be cautious about exposing themselves to criticism by giving favorable publicity to controversial causes. Reporters and rewrite men have the same fear of provoking criticism by their superiors. You have to let them off the hook by providing a legitimate news peg around which your case can be outlined or at least brought to repetitive public attention.

Unless such a peg exists, create it. The pseudo-event is one of the mainstays of modern politics and social innovation. When you have something to say to the public, make it news by saying it instead to an arranged gathering, even if that gathering consists only of your already loyal supporters, all of whom have heard it before.

Provide the journalists (and your news releases) with the conventional who-what-when-where-why-how. Not "The Human Relations Council claimed today that deplorable housing conditions in this city are blighting the lives of hundreds of children," but "John Jones, president of the Human Relations Council, told a meeting of concerned citizens at the High School Auditorium last night that deplorable housing conditions in this city are blighting the lives . . . , etc." Now the editor is confronted with a fact, an actual event (the meeting), rather than a mere opinion; he is far more likely to consider it news and far less vulnerable to criticism if he uses it. Thus he's more likely to use it.

Another form of pseudo-event which lends news value to your public statements is the directing of those statements to important public officials. "A delegation of citizens headed by John Jones, president of the Human Relations Council, appealed today to Mayor Thomas Anderson and the City Housing Authority to double the number of public housing units to be made available to low-income families next year. . . . The group presented Mayor Anderson and the five-member CHA with photographs of rats feeding in alleyways, small children crowded four to a bed . . . , etc." And make sure the press gets copies of these photographs! With this tactic you've combined a series of news elements (a specific event, a newsworthy personality, visual evidence) which will be hard for an editor to resist.

Both research reports and progress reports can be occasions for news releases which bring your efforts once more to public attention. But to get the best results, arrange to make such reports to someone, rather than simply releasing them to the press. Their presentation at meetings—even small subcommittee or executive board meetings—lends them a factual news basis which editors will welcome.

Political candidates in major campaigns use advance texts of the speeches they're supposedly giving in this manner. Often the candidate's actual remarks at a semi-formal appearance may bear only casual resemblance to the text released to the press. In person, the candidate may concentrate on localized, topical remarks calculated to please the particular crowd, yet his advance press release has put into the record more studied statements which he wishes to expose to a wider public. Few newsmen are actually present, so most published reports are based on the carefully planned news release rather than the informal performance which actually took place.

The author recalls a congressional candidate who got excellent press coverage by using even small, semi-private coffee klatches as news release events in which major position statements could be revealed to the general public through the press. "Representative Smith told a meeting of Centerville citizens last night that . . . , etc." On one occasion, nobody showed up except the hostess, who already knew the candidate's position on all major issues; they exchanged personal small talk over coffee, but meanwhile, in newspaper composing rooms, the advance news release about the candidate's intended remarks was taken at face value. The next morning the press of his district gave top billing to a talk which had never actually been delivered.

We are not proposing that you hoodwink the press; our point is simply that the news release which conveys your statements to a large audience is a more important communications vehicle than the actual words you speak to a small group. But the existence of that small group—providing a forum for making your statement or presenting your report to actual people in a newsworthy setting—greatly increases the prospect that editors and broadcasters will relay your message to their larger audiences.

Unless your project is one of earthshaking significance or very high drama, you will seldom see newspaper or broadcast reporters. Large metropolitan media have too many choices to enable them to cover in person any except the most newsworthy. Small local media seldom have staffs for more than a bare minimum of on-the-spot coverage. So both lean primarily on what you tell them happened.

Build into your publicity program some specific devices to inspire the confidence of the press. First, make it apparent that you would welcome their direct coverage, that things are going to happen as you've said they are, that you have nothing to hide. You can accomplish this by distributing advance schedule memoranda, informing the press of each anticipated event which might provide news. You can do it by sending advance news releases—postdated stories written far enough in advance (about events and statements which you can safely predict will become facts) so that the press has the story before the event occurs and thus has an opportunity to come and check its veracity if it wishes.

Confidence can be inspired by adding to every news release a name and telephone number which the press can call to verify the information or expand upon it. The author can personally testify that in scores of such instances, when the verification name on the release was his, he was never called for such verification except in rare instances when an editor wanted to expand on a particular aspect of the story by obtaining more information. The point is that your mere willingness to verify a story is normally all the verification the press requires.

The enclosure of supporting documents, which provide an editor with the broad background context of your news release, can also help inspire press confidence. A story highlighting the most dramatic evidence presented by your researchers to an organizational meeting, or to a public agency during the pre-organizational publicity campaign, should include a copy of the full research report. The announcement of your candidacy for a public office should include a biographical summary. Announcements of technically complex plans should be accompanied by detailed feasibility studies or technical proposals prepared by the businesses which hope to sell you their services or equipment. The editor may never read these lengthy supporting documents, but their presence—your obvious willingness to have them read —testifies to the validity of your news release summaries.

The quality of journalism and photography displayed by

your releases will also have a significant bearing on their use. This is particularly true of small, understaffed local news media. In many cases, the quality of their own journalism is incredibly bad, and the editor knows it; he simply can't afford the talent to do anything about it. When your releases are well written, professionally styled, such editors are often delighted to display them prominently because they appear in the paper as though his own staff prepared them. The same can be said of photographs which display imaginative composition, dramatic angles, near-live action.

Few assets will serve your project as well as competent journalistic recruits. They are worth specialized and concentrated attention during recruitment, especially during the preorganizational stage, when the big story of your formal establishment is being planned and polished for that all-important first impression on the public.

But beware of overly aggressive publicists. As their fervor for gaining news space grows, whetted by early success, they may lose sight of the fact that tactics which excite the media may not always serve your interests. They can put you out on an embarrassing limb by dangerously projecting early results from a survey or petition drive or fund drive or opinion poll; this creates expectations of later results which you may not be able to fulfill, and such a failure will be widely interpreted as a loss of momentum, a weakening of support, a flagging of interest.

Publicists are particularly prone to use the drama of attack against newsworthy individuals as a sure key to headlines. They know you'll get twice the space by presenting your report to the mayor as a bold and belligerent demonstration than by presenting it as a cordial visit and a civil exchange of views. Attacking the mayor multiplies news value, because it draws his own political position, as well as yours, into the picture.

But attacking the mayor also mobilizes his supporters into automatic opposition, even though they may be essentially unconcerned about your project. (And you have to assume that the mayor, or any elected official, has a lot of friends; otherwise he wouldn't be where he is.) The pointless stirring of hornets' nests may be good journalism, but it is seldom good politics.

Establish clearly understood guidelines, then, for the supervision of publicity. Certain leeway must be granted for fast, factual releases on such events as late night meetings without holding up work for cumbersome clearance processes. But where particularly crucial releases are involved, you might revert to that "What if?" review technique we've used previously. Show the story to the executive board, and brainstorm its implications and probable results.

Publicity is not only a disseminator of information, it is also a good source of information. Research analysis of the comparative press space devoted to you and to your opponent in a political campaign and careful monitoring of all opposition publicity are essentials of sound campaigning. Summaries of such analyses should be circulated among your leadership group (don't assume everybody reads everything in the local press) and among your publicity team, to show them what they are achieving and what gaps they need to fill.

Spot polls and surveys can also provide valuable feedback on the effectiveness of your publicity. But make certain your samples are large enough and your methods are sound enough to lend validity to the results. The combination of slanted polls and wishful thinking has led many a campaign toward unpleasant surprises.

CHAPTER TWELVE

Fund raising

Your campaign budget may vary from a few dollars for incidental expenses to thousands of dollars for metropolitan media political advertising or mass production printing. If you're attempting to achieve your aims through a privately financed co-operative venture, fund raising may even be the major purpose of your campaign, rather than an incidental necessity.

Fund raising is a productive use of campaign personnel whenever it expands the organization's capabilities faster than it uses them up (in manpower, money, etc.) Being able to afford to rent an empty storefront or office for a few months, for a campaign headquarters, will almost certainly get extra man-hours out of your volunteers because they'll be more likely to devote spare time to some place which is "theirs" than they will to get together for work sessions under conditions which require someone to be the host and others to suspect that they might be intruding or imposing.

The ready availability of simple office supplies will speed the flow of productive work. A special telephone, and a roster schedule for manning it, will facilitate communication by giving everyone a known point of contact. You may even find that hiring a part-time secretary will relieve volunteers of dull tasks which sap their enthusiasm. Being able to afford to print basic literature as a back-up for face-to-face campaigning will improve the impact of your quickly recruited, amateur organization.

If your budget is nominal, the easiest way to raise it is by modest membership dues or by passing the hat at meetings. But even for fifty dollars (which an adept panhandler can raise on the streets without the backing of a good cause), amateur organizations have a propensity for going about fund raising the hard way.

Rummage sales, talent or fashion shows, formal dinners

or lectures for ticket purchasers, are standard features of civic improvement campaigns. Frequently, the manpower invested in them is too high a price to pay for the nominal funds they raise.

Such fund-raising sales—of tickets, rummage, or what-not—are popular not because they're the most effective way to get people to contribute money, but because the fund raisers themselves are more comfortable selling than they are soliciting. Our folk mores are such that we feel honorbound to make some symbolic exchange, to give people something immediate and concrete for their money, even when the donors would rather not be bothered by having to haul the junk home or devote an evening to a stuffy dinner or a dull lecture.

This is not to deny that such activities have beneficial side effects. Frequently they involve people who would not be willing to undertake other tasks in the campaign; again, the more people you can involve, the better off you are. And they generate incidental publicity which helps keep your project in the public mind. But unless such events are very well planned and superbly executed, they are unlikely to raise significant sums for an extensive budget, and the leadership and talents which go into such excellent planning and performance can usually be put to better use elsewhere.

Be willing to take advantage of the fact that your community improvement project can, if it succeeds, produce real benefits for a large segment of the local population. Spell out the benefits, both in terms of dollars (the elimination of public costs now stemming from the problem you hope to solve, or the economic or property value impact of the improvement you seek) and in terms of human values.

Make your appeal for significant contributions on the basis of this straightforward justification. Sell the project itself, not irrelevant merchandise or amateur entertainment. Ask for direct contributions.

This direct approach enables you to combine fund raising with effective campaigning. People soliciting contributions frequently communicate even more intensely than those seeking vague commitments of political support because, again, our folk mores press us to prove that the contributor is getting his money's worth. Even when such a solicitation fails to produce a contribution, it accomplishes all the informational and persuasive purposes of campaigning.

Before you begin soliciting funds, check into the legal requirements for reporting contributions and dispersements. Particularly in the case of political campaigns, these regulations are usually specific and sometimes complex. The town or city clerk's office is the place to start; the municipal legal counsel may be of assistance; your legislators will tell you about state and federal requirements.

By all means establish a bank account at the beginning of your project and make sure every cent you take in or spend goes through that account. Even when the amount of money involved is nominal, banks are very willing to serve community organizations in this respect as a public relations gesture. The bank account gives you accurate, verified records and makes it easy to pay suppliers by check rather than having to keep up with who advanced what from his own pocket.

With any legal requirements regarding public solicitation met, and a bank account to put your money in, you're now ready to start. There are three basic forms of direct solicitation—mail, the telephone, and face-to-face requests. Mail is easiest, but generally least effective. The telephone is a time-saving compromise. Face-to-face solicitation is by far the most productive approach.

For any of these approaches, you must identify an audience and provide that audience with essential background information. That card file you started back in preorganization days, the indications of interest you noted during any advance surveys or while inviting people to the organizational meeting, or simply the personal knowledge you and your leadership group have of the financial circumstances and community interests of a large number of people will produce a "prospect list."

Previous political candidates whose positions were similar to yours will have filed official reports of contributors, and those reports are generally public records which you can consult. People who've worked in other fund drives often know who's susceptible to a worthy request for financial assistance. Sometimes other organizations can be approached for funds. Remember that corporations are generally prohibited from making political contributions, but labor unions are not, and labor unions are frequently sympathetic to projects which have as their goal broad community benefits.

But by far the best prospect list you'll ever build will be your own membership roster. The general public is subjected to many seemingly worthwhile appeals for money. The people most likely to single out your appeal are those who already have a stake in its success—the committed members of your organization.

In fact, this psychology should be put to good use in recruiting personnel for your fund drive. You've no doubt noticed that churches and philanthropies generally name their most affluent members as leaders in their fund campaigns, even when they have to create titles for these people. Not only does their resulting ego stake in the success of the drive influence their own contributions; the fact that they make generous contributions themselves makes them less hesitant to ask others to do likewise.

But when you recruit such people for leading fund drive assignments, be careful not to sap the vigor of that drive by loading your chain of command with affluent but ineffective personnel. Create honorary or advisory roles for any you suspect might lack force and persistence and commitment in organized activity.

Generally, then, the people from whom you can hope to raise money fall within four categories—the fund-raising team itself, the rest of your campaign organization or membership, accumulatively developed lists of good prospects outside the organization, and the general public.

What you can expect from each category will depend on the nature of your project and the nature of the community. If your goal is a widely desired one, appeals to the general public through systematic door-to-door solicitations can be profitable. If your proposal is controversial, or creates little interest, such general appeals are likely to be disappointing; people will decline because the contribution, even if they can easily afford it, associates them with a cause which has not yet gained respectability.

In an affluent neighborhood almost anyone can afford a hundred dollars for a good cause, if he can be persuaded that the cause is urgent. Thus it is likely that your general membership can afford to finance the campaign without going to the public. In a low-income neighborhood, the small size of average donations may well force you to go door-to-door for a large number of such donations or to lean primarily on a well-prepared list of special prospects, perhaps philanthropically inclined people from outside the community.

But in this prosperous society of ours, it is surprisingly easy to talk a substantial number of people out of a hundred dollars or more. All that's required is careful preparation of your audience, some special effort to get them involved, and a direct request with persistent follow-up.

Preparation means the distribution of appropriate information. You not only have to demonstrate that your cause is worth the money; you have to provide evidence that the money will be well spent. This involves letting prospective contributors in on all but the most confidential details of your campaign plan.

Few devices can accomplish this as effectively as a good campaign newsletter—one for insiders, as opposed to the external newsletter we discussed earlier for publicity purposes. Consider adding significant prospects for financial support to your mailing list, whether they've joined the organization or not.

Another means of attuning potentially major contributors to your cause and your needs is to ask for their advice— about anything plausible which involves a thorough explanation of your project. You can get a head start in those final days just before the organizational meeting if you already have a list of possibilities. Assign each member of the steering committee to make several contacts. Phone and ask permission to come talk about an important new community project, explaining that you are not seeking any commitment or open support (that can come later), but merely want to collect ideas, especially about people who might be invited to the organizational meeting. (Without pushing them, of course, you'll want to include them in that invitation.)

Later you might draw such prospects into your enterprise by asking them to suggest others who might contribute. Or you might ask if they know of people who would be willing to host fund-raising events such as dinners or parties for your prospect list.

Bide your time during these early contacts. Don't ask for money and don't push too hard for open commitments of support. But immediately add each person you talk with in this matter to your newsletter mailing list. When the time comes for a direct solicitation, they'll practically be members of the family.

Whatever approach you take, a good fund-raising prospectus is an absolute necessity. It shouldn't be too wordy, but it should make the case for your cause in the strongest possible terms. It should convince readers that your project is feasible, that their money has a good chance to accomplish something important. And it should explain enough about how that money is to be used to demonstrate that you really need it and know how to make the most of it.

Another good way to soften up a list of prospective contributors is to entertain them by providing a humorous warning of your intentions—and then dazzling them with a series of subsequent communications which build to a climax. For example:

The first note, mailed with your fund raising prospectus, simply says: "One hundred people in this city have got to shell out $100 apiece to open a new community center that will keep West Side kids out of jail. A fellow in a white hat told us you were a good guy—so I assume you're going to be one of that hundred. Stand by for more information."

The very next day, the same list of prospects get a second note—and another copy of the prospectus. This one says: "Oops! Yesterday I forgot to tell you that while you're standing by for more information, you should read our fund drive prospectus. In case you've misplaced it, here's another one. That part about each kid who's sent to jail costing us $19,000 in tax money each *year, for prison costs, is true. So the $10,000 we need to start a West Side community center to keep scores of kids off the streets is really quite a bargain."*

Mailing notes daily for a week or so will make it impossible for any of your best several dozen prospects to ignore you. The sense of humor will make it difficult for any to resent you. Such brief cover notes can be handwritten for personal impact. Then, when you suspect the game has gone on long enough— bang! Phone for an appointment, or call unannounced if you really want to outmaneuver alibis, and ask for your money. You'll be surprised how much you'll get.

By whatever process you've softened them up, the surest way to get your prospects to come across is to involve them actively in your project—preferably in the fund-raising drive itself. For instance, recruit people to give parties for other people who might also be willing to give parties. Don't ask for contributions at these parties; ask each guest to agree to give a similar party. By the time they've helped as a host, their sympathies are engaged. Wait a week, and then make a personal request for their contribution. Keep following up the chain of hosts recruited by each party in the same manner. (Those who attend a party but decline to give one can, of course, be asked for a contribution immediately; their refusal to work may have created a guilt feeling which they'll salve by generosity in contributing.)

You might recruit prospective contributors to help prepare the fund-raising prospectus; you might put them to work writing more of those cute little notes; there are all kinds of things they can do. But the backbone of any fund drive is its actual solicitors. This is the work you want to ask any who are willing to do, because it's probably the hardest work to get people to do in any volunteer organization.

We've noted before that there are three basic ways to ask people for contributions—by mail, by phone, and in person.

Mail is the most difficult, in terms of results, though it is perhaps easiest in terms of execution. However, even though you may not count on the mail to produce much actual cash, it can play a very important part in conditioning prospects to respond to more personal appeals. The newsletter mailings and the series of humorous notes mentioned previously are cases in point.

Any organization which expects to raise a significant amount of money should obtain two things from the post office promptly: a box number, and a business reply permit. Post office boxes can be rented for a dollar or so a month. Such a box gives you a permanent address—the box number—where contributions will be secure until it is convenient to pick them up and deposit them in the bank.

A business reply permit, which costs nothing, is simply post office permission to print reply envelopes which require no postage from the contributor; you pay the postage when you receive them at the post office. Postage costs will not be excessive, because you're only paying for those which come back, and most of them contain checks. Your business reply envelopes (which must be printed according to an official design; any post office and almost any printer has a sample) make it easy for contributors to write spur-of-the-moment checks. They don't have to figure out where to send them, address an envelope, or find a stamp; they simply insert the check, seal, and mail.

One technicality which is too often forgotten in fund solicitations is how to make out the check. Since yours is probably a newly formed organization, many people will be uncertain as to its exact name. Always include this information in your fund-raising letters, on your prospectus, and in such widely disseminated communications as your newsletter.

If you hope to use mail to raise anything more than small contributions, start early and be persistent. Plan a continuing series of mailings to your prime prospect list; keep your letters brief and interesting, with a steady flow of new information which will ward off boredom. Leave it to enclosures (the fund prospectus or other literature) to spell things out for those who want all the details. Include a reply envelope with every mailing; they'll only cost about a penny apiece and you can afford to invest several dollars in the pursuit of hundred-dollar-or-more contributions.

You'll improve results if you'll use the mail to disseminate background information, and then use the telephone to clinch the deal. The mail preparation—and whatever else you've done to make prospects aware of the need by involving them in your venture—will eliminate lengthy telephone explanations and deprive the prospect of that deadly alibi: "I'll need time to think it over."

When solicitors follow up by phone, they should have a brief and pat speech ready; otherwise they'll get caught up in hemming and hawing and be much less forceful than they should. For example:

"Mrs. Smith, this is Oscar Brown from the Montague-for-Mayor Campaign. As you know, Tom Montague is primarily concerned about the lack of long-range planning here in town and his election could prevent some very serious problems in the next few years. Tom is making a personal sacrifice by running for this office and his opposition is spending a lot of money to keep him out of City Hall. We need to raise $5,000 promptly to support his campaign plans. We're hoping we can find fifty people who'll contribute a hundred dollars each. Would you be one of them?"

This is about the maximum length for such a telephone presentation; if your preliminary mailings have adequately prepared the ground, you can leave out such background information as the second and third sentences. The idea is to identify yourself and your cause clearly—to allay any suspicions—and then ask directly for a contribution, before the prospect says anything except "Hello." Without such a prepared pitch, the prospect is likely to realize what is coming during the preliminaries, and outmaneuver the solicitor with alibis before the key question is asked.

Note the specific reference to a hundred dollars; you'll recall that we've used it in other examples. If you do not cite a specific amount, prospects will get rid of you quickly by volunteering nominal sums, and you'll be in the position of having to express gratitude for peanuts when you really expected gold nuggets.

If you have a few special prospects whom you suspect

are worth more than a hundred dollars, develop a separate approach for them. Certainly you'd never leave such solicitations to the mail or phone; they deserve a personal visit in any kind of campaign. Instead of specifying an amount, you merely say: "We need every cent we can get our hands on, and hope we can count on you for some important financial support." Let them take it from there.

But for most people who're likely to end up on a hand-picked financial prospect list, a hundred dollars is possible if they're sufficiently committed; and you're not likely to get much more under normal circumstances. By picking a specific, significant amount like this, you discourage people who can afford generosity from buying you off with token contributions; they may not give you a hundred dollars, but you'll get more twenty-fives than fives with this approach.

When you use the telephone for such solicitations, you should secure your gains with a quick mail follow-up. Before concluding your telephone conversation, you should have explained how the check should be made out and where it should be sent. But if you'll immediately write a brief note repeating this information, and enclosing one of those preaddressed reply envelopes, you'll be much more likely to get your money, and get it promptly.

One standard phenomenon of telephone soliciting will also give you problems in face-to-face fund raising; this phenomenon is the impact of refusals on your volunteer solicitors.

People who turn you down are going to feel a bit guilty about doing so, and they'll allay that guilt, in many cases, with displays of hostility. Your solicitors will be told that their cause is a fraud, their leader a charlatan, and they themselves prime examples of unmitigated gall. A volunteer may withstand one hostile rejection, but after two or three, he dreads going back to that telephone. He takes a break; and procrastination multiplies his tension. If he does eventually force himself back into action, his solicitations may be almost apologetic and any semi-hesitant prospect will slip quickly through his grasp.

We've talked earlier about pairing volunteers to overcome such sensitivity to rejections in door-to-door campaigning; the same thing can work here. You may have to prod people a bit to get them to do it, since telephone calls are normally made in private and it only takes one person to carry a check after a personal visit. But such explanations as "We can learn from each other if we work in teams," or "People will be less likely to display their stinginess to two people than to one" will help you pull it off.

But the most direct answer is that prepared pitch. Whether you're making it by phone or face-to-face, it should follow the same pattern illustrated above: clear identification, brief background, specific amount a bit higher than the prospect probably expects (unless you're fishing for a very large donation), and direct request—all bang, bang, bang, before the prospect has a chance to put up defenses. Then let the conversation follow a normal course, but always end it with a specific "What have you decided?"

Point out frankly to solicitors their own probable reaction to rejections and hostility; make a joke of it if you can. But then remind them that almost anyone can survive several hours of discomfort, if need be, for a cause as good as yours, and ask them to agree to make all of the contacts on their list in a specific, fairly brief period of time. Assure them that if they'll simply hold their breath and dive in, they'll have some pleasant experiences along with the uncomfortable ones; many a fund drive solicitor finds himself plied with cocktails and delightful conversation as well as money.

And remember that no matter how well you use them, mail and phone solicitations are never as effective as properly executed face-to-face requests. Some people give eagerly, yet most, even though they're sympathetic and able to afford it, would just as soon you'd called on someone else. But they give, because they can't bring themselves to admit that they're not one of the "good guys" and our pride in affluence makes them hesitant about claiming they don't have the money.

It's easy to reject an envelope; you simply throw it in the wastebasket. It's a bit more difficult to reject a voice on the phone, particularly if it's someone you know, but at least you don't have to look it in the eyes or escort it awkwardly to the door after you've said no. It's much, much harder to reject a sincere, dedicated, public-spirited citizen who is a momentary guest in your home or office, and that's precisely why face-to-face solicitation yields the best results. Otherwise, the face-to-face approach is very similar to the telephone approach already outlined.

You may be able to improve the returns from either approach—or for that matter, from mail solicitations—by starting early and asking for pledges instead of cash. (If you do it by phone, fill out a pledge form for the agreed amount and mail a confirmation copy; when the time comes to collect, people may not remember purely verbal pledges as serious commitments.)

Remember that the scope—and the success or failure— of a fund drive has a significant psychological impact on both your organization and the general public. Obviously you need a goal to enable you to evaluate progress. Normally that goal would be the total amount of your budget. But people are likely to relax as they approach such a goal, and this relaxation may cause the drive to fall short. This may disrupt your entire plan of operations. So it's wise to pad the budget with a layer of desirable but unnecessary spending plans which can be eliminated without serious disruption, if you fall short.

On the other hand, setting a high goal and falling a bit short can create a public impression of lack of support and momentum and can cripple the morale of your volunteers. Some organizations guard against this by being vague about goals or secretive about results. Such deceptions can create unnecessary complications and even serious suspicions.

The best compromise is probably that of publicizing your goal only to those people involved in the fund drive and those on your list of serious prospects. If you fall short, the negative impact will be limited because only a small portion of the community is aware of the failure. The general public, from whom you expect only nominal contributions, can be kept interested by what appears to be an open-ended campaign, and whatever results you achieve can be labeled a victory.

CHAPTER THIRTEEN

Controlling the campaign organization

No matter how well your steering committee has planned the campaign, no matter how successful your recruiters have been, there will come times when you're certain that the order of the day is the one widely known among political campaigners as Murphy's Law: "Whatever can go wrong will go wrong."

A volunteer community campaign is, in some ways, more difficult to manage than a full-time business or other organization. Its participants are not in constant communication. They do not work in terms of "real time": it may take a week to finish a five-hour job because the person performing it is only available two evenings during the week. Throughout the organization, communications are complicated because people know each other only casually and thus are less able to interpret nuances than they would be in a full-time operation.

As we've pointed out before, planning your campaign so that it is divided into several distinct phases will enable you to shift people in search of the most effective combination under these circumstances.

We've already suggested that you build into your campaign plan a very early phase of public activity (right after the organizational meeting) which gives you an opportunity to watch every new recruit in action. A door-to-door opinion survey, petition drive, or literature distribution provides a simple, straightforward task which accomplishes this purpose. But whatever device you use, it should be an undertaking which, while helpful to the over-all campaign, is not absolutely essential or decisive. For in this "trial run" you'll discover quite a few ineffective people who need to be reassigned before the major thrust of your campaign is undertaken.

125

How do you discover such people, and what do you do about them?

The key to personnel evaluation—and, in fact, just about the only means of discipline—in a volunteer organization is the progress report. What people *can't* tell you in such prearranged progress reports is often as significant in identifying poor leadership and weak performance as what they do tell you. And the knowledge that they definitely are going to be asked for specific progress reports is the strongest discipline in the organization; few will wish to expose their egos to confessions of "no progress."

Discipline most often breaks down when progress report requirements are vague. It can also be undermined by the natural (and otherwise commendable) compassion of volunteer supervisors for embarrassed or insecure workers, if it prevents them from insisting on complete and specific information whenever a helper feels awkward about having failed. For example:

You're conducting an opinion survey to prove to the City Council that taxpayers are willing to spend more money on services to youth and would approve of the addition of a properly trained youth officer to the police force. You've divided the city into areas, and each Area Chairman has two teams of five door-to-door opinion surveyors, each recruited and supervised by a Team Leader.

In the five areas of the city, you hope to survey 1,000 families—or 200 families per area—in one weekend. You've announced in advance that Area Chairmen are expected to report to you on Saturday evening, halfway through the weekend, so that remedial steps can be taken if the goal isn't at least half accomplished.

Your Area Three chairman reports a specific total of 113 families interviewed. He's talked to both of his Team Leaders. The first reported definite totals for four canvassers and a definite zero for the fifth (who despite her earlier commitment, decided to paint the kitchen that Saturday). The second Team Leader has totals from two canvassers, but reports that he "couldn't make contact" with the other three. The Area Chairman has placed zeroes beside those three names.

What have you learned from this progress report?

First, it's obvious that you have a reasonably good chairman in Area Three; he's got two Team Leaders functioning; at the halfway point he's achieved more than half of his goal; he's realistic enough to assume no progress where none can be proved.

You have an excellent leader for the first team. He knows exactly what's happened, and he got 80 per cent performance from his canvassers (not bad at this early stage). Start considering this fellow for a bigger job in the next phase of the campaign.

Your second Team Leader is willing but weak. He thought he had five canvassers, and he probably went through the proper basic motions, because two of them knew enough to function. But he doesn't really know what happened; either his control was so loose that three canvassers ignored the timetable, or he himself is so reticent or weakly motivated that he made only a superficial effort to contact them for progress reports. By all means continue to use this willing volunteer, but keep an eye on him and consider shifting him from a command position to doorbell ringing in the next phase.

That lady in the first team who painted her kitchen instead of making her appointed rounds may be a woman's club officer whom you had in mind for a key job in the next phase. Now you've got to reassess her dependability.

Meanwhile, Area Five reports only twenty-two signatures collected. The first Team Leader had only recruited two of his five canvassers, but he says he'll go out himself on Sunday and help them meet the team's quota. The second Team Leader was out of town, and the Area Chairman doesn't know who her canvassers are, so no progress report can be obtained. But the chairman estimates that if two canvassers got twenty-two signatures for the first team, five should have collected at least fifty for Team Two, so things are not too bad. When you asked whether the Team One leader had been instructed to get busy recruiting more canvassers for Sunday, the chairman explained that this leader was hesitant about taking the job in the beginning and any such pressure might cause him to quit.

You've got big trouble in Area Five. The chairman has

obviously failed to maintain regular communication with the Team Leaders; otherwise, he'd know who at least some of those Team Two canvassers are. The chairman has allowed an obvious weak spot to develop by putting a superficially committed person (the Team One leader) in a crucial position and is now too soft to cope with that weakness by pushing for a fulfillment of commitments. The Team One leader probably wouldn't be too good even if he were more committed, because he prefers foot-soldiering (collecting signatures himself) to leadership (recruiting those extra canvassers to fill out the campaign organization).

You've got to suspect that Team Two leader—until evidence develops that she actually did have five canvassers and had made certain they'd do their jobs before she left town—but she could still turn out to be the best thing you've got in Area Five.

This situation illustrates the necessity for back-up forces during the vital stages of any campaign. If you have a "floating" canvass team awaiting assignment, you can throw them into Area Five on Sunday to meet the goal, whatever the existing area organization does. If you have a flexible troubleshooter in the wings, you can push the Area Five chairman hard for specific assurances that the situation will be corrected promptly. When you get the predictable alibis ("I've already promised my wife a family picnic on Sunday and I've got a rush job at the office for the next few days"), you should simply restate the importance of keeping the campaign on schedule, and then ask the reluctant chairman if he'd mind someone else moving in and doing the job, with assurances that you'll find a later or less-demanding role for him. Then send your troubleshooter into the breech until you find a replacement.

You've just been through the very subtle exercise of firing a volunteer. The same result can be achieved by continuing to press the nonperformer hard enough so that he'll quit of his own accord. Too often, however, people feel the need to justify such retreats by shifting blame to others and estranging themselves from the campaign or joining the opposition. So it's better to propose the move yourself, diplomatically, by providing welcome relief before it is demanded.

Now think back over the examples in these last few

pages, and bear in mind that all of the evaluations we've discussed stemmed from brief phone conversations between you and two Area Chairmen. The whole process took perhaps ten minutes. In thirty minutes you could talk with all five Area Chairmen and get the same insight into the functioning of your entire campaign organization. Furthermore, the mere fact that those chairmen know you're going to call them again the next night for a full weekend progress report will stimulate considerable activity over the next twenty-four hours.

But it won't work unless the goals are specific and the progress reports have been adequately announced in advance. Don't announce them as indications of insecurity—as suspicious opportunities to check up on people; find more acceptable reasons. The necessity for knowing where your reserve forces can best be employed is one such reason; the possibility of turning early results into useful publicity is another.

In a big organization, you might wish to verify the progress report chain of communications with some independent check of your own. This will smoke out problems that others prefer to hide and give you a better feel for the grass roots of your organization. You can do this by touring the community during periods of peak activity and talking with your front-line performers, and then comparing what you've seen with the reports you receive through the chain of command. Or you can use people other than your command chain to collect reports farther down the pyramid by intensive telephoning at agreed times ("We'll call every Team Leader from headquarters, between six and seven Saturday evening"). These independent progress checkers may give you a more objective picture of your organization than the Area Chairmen could; the Area Chairmen will accept this intervention if it is presented as a time-saving aid to them and a means of getting quick information in a brief time span.

One congressional election campaign with some 3,000 volunteers used student aides for this purpose. These aides were given the names of campaign coordinators in thirty-one cities or towns. With a battery of four phones, a team of students working after classes was able to contact each grass roots coordinator over a two-day period, assembling information which was then chan-

neled back to regional and city chairmen to show them where their weak spots were, but was also used by the campaign manager to select assignments for the floating reserves.

Thus, deliberate phasing of your campaign provides the opportunity for reassigning people to achieve a steadily improving organization and regular, preannounced progress reports (based on specific, quantitative measurements of what has been done, rather than opinions or estimates of the quality of performance) provide not only subtle discipline but the information on which you can base sound personnel assignments.

But neither will accomplish their purposes unless you use the opportunity which the phase changes offer for making such personnel shifts. Particularly where your long-time friends are involved, you may be reluctant to demote people who clearly consider themselves leaders and want to be close to the center of the campaign.

Often you'll find it possible to create advisory assignments which preserve the prestige of your original leaders while enabling you to remove them from the direct chain of command (where their shortcomings affect not only their own tasks, but coordinated efforts of others) and make room for newer, more effective recruits. The personal politics of such situations is easier if you build such advisory councils or review committees into the organization chart during the preliminary planning stage, so they don't seem to have been created as graveyards for "old elephants."

These advisory groups can actually serve a useful purpose. They provide a double check on the perspectives of operational leaders (including you) who are caught up in the pressures of deadlines and coordinated work schedules and inevitable minor crises.

But such advisory groups should be kept out of the chain of command and should operate independently of the timetable. Don't assign them tasks which can delay other operations; don't let them make decisions which you'll be obliged to follow.

One of the trickier aspects of organizational leadership is that of soliciting advice and ideas without becoming obliged to accept them. The simplest way to stay out of such a corner is to turn an unacceptable idea back on its sponsor. Point out that the regular organizational plan is already using all of your available manpower. Ask the proponent of such an idea how he or she would go about carrying it out without disrupting the basic plan. Then—unless it is such a bad idea that it could have a negative effect if carried out—let the proponent go off on his own and have a try at it. He'll be out of your way, and nothing is lost if he fails.

Unfortunately, in the case of a political campaign, candidates are faced with many suggestions as to what they should say about specific issues which conflict with their own convictions, and these are often accompanied by threatening implications that the proponent may abandon the cause or join the opposition unless the candidate agrees. In these cases, the best thing you can do is to invite the proponent to prepare a carefully documented study report. If it is produced quickly, ask questions until you find reasons for requesting additional research. Sooner or later your self-appointed advisor will tire of the game, without being able to say that you were unwilling to listen, or that you pointedly refused to take his suggestion.

Just as you channel weak members of your original leadership into nondisruptive roles by kicking them upstairs to advisory posts outside the operational chain of command, you should also keep the campaign's specialists outside that chain of command. Make sure that such across-the-board functions as publicity, research, central administration, and (except when it is the main business of the campaign) fund raising function apart from the mass manpower chain of command, so that general operations are not delayed by their special requirements. But by all means maintain regular communication between the specialized functions and the general command structure, so they can coordinate efforts, take advantage of each other's information, and continually refine their respective roles as members of a team.

The same separation of command should be maintained for parallel aspects of the major campaign. Don't delegate to the same individual the responsibility for preparing material for a petition drive and recruiting and organizing the canvassers. Let each function proceed independently—so that problems and delays in one will not affect the other—until the moment when they must come together: the day you place the material in the hands of the canvassers.

Specialization of functions achieves specialization of decision making. When two functions are combined under the same supervision, the people involved in both most get together to make plans or decisions about either. This can double the amount of time each individual must devote to meetings and reduce the time all can therefore contribute to the actual work at hand.

You should retain a certain amount of flexibility about revising your basic campaign plan, your budget, or your schedule as the project unfolds. Each phase will teach you things you didn't know during the preliminary planning period. Use your scheduled phase changes as occasions for review and adjustment. For instance:

Your original plan called for a public opinion survey shortly after the organizational meeting, to set the stage for a big "Mothers' Protest" demonstration in front of City Hall concerning inadequate public housing. Despite advance publicity, your organizational meeting was lightly attended, suggesting that public concern was not of enormous proportions. Your survey indicated that a large majority of housewives did consider the city's housing program inadequate, but very few except in slum areas were upset enough to join an organization or demonstrate publicly to attempt to change the situation. How does this affect your plans?

It's now probable that your City Hall demonstration will be embarrassingly weak—that it may, in fact, defeat your purposes by revealing to the authorities something they may not have known: that people are not sufficiently disturbed to present a political threat. But you've also learned that a well-worded petition expressing discontent with the city housing program and requesting remedial action could gain the approval of such a large number of voters that City Hall might be frightened (politically) into taking the action you desire. As you conclude the survey phase, then, it makes obvious sense to adjust your plans—to convert the energy and manpower you were going to devote to organizing a demonstration into the new channel of a petition drive.

These changes of plans and reassignments of personnel, plus the constant addition of new recruits, require a continuing communications effort. Unless the entire organization is kept abreast of all such developments, and unless newcomers are quickly brought to the same state of understanding as the previous arrivals, wasted motion and duplication of efforts will sap your resources and destroy the group's morale.

The normal chain of command will also function naturally as a chain of communication. In theory you can disseminate information quickly to a large organization by simply giving it to your top-echelon leaders, and asking them to pass it on to the next echelon, who will in turn do likewise. If you've maintained short spans of control in your organizational chart, no one will have to make more than a few phone calls. It works just like a chain letter.

But recall that old parlor game in which all the participants sit side by side in a long line. The first one whispers a message to the next, who passes it on to the next, etc. The entire point of the game is that when the last person repeats the message aloud its original content will have changed significantly. A phenomenon which is a source of humor at a party can be a very frustrating, disruptive element in a public campaign.

When the project organization is small, regular meetings of the full membership can supplement chain-of-command communication and bring everybody up-to-date with an accurate picture of plans and progress. But even in a small group, remember that meetings take up time which members would otherwise be willing to devote to the actual work of the campaign.

The efforts of your publicity team will also serve to keep your organization informed; the public may pay only superficial attention to the details you report, but they will have added significance for your own members. In fact, a good part of the value of publicity is its impact on your already committed recruits, because they will be the most attentive audience for the press and broadcast reports you inspire.

Where the fast flow of information through a large organization is required, you might try that same special telephone team (including the possibility of those student aides) which was suggested as a means of getting reliable progress reports. In fact, all formal progress report arrangements should be two-way communications channels, with the leadership providing information for workers at the same time it requests their progress reports.

But after all this is said and done, special consideration should be given in any campaign of significant scope, any organization of more than a handful of people, to the distribution of an official campaign newsletter. In many cases only the individual at the top knows everything, because only there does the communication pyramid flow into a single point. And it is the people nearest the top who best understand the over-all campaign—what is important and what is superficial, what priorities should be observed, and what problems should be anticipated.

The organizational newsletter enables this top leadership to communicate with everyone with a minimum of effort. It has the further advantage of making certain that everyone gets exactly the same information—a valuable aid to coordination. And it provides information in a form which members can retain for future reference.

Furthermore, a newsletter greatly reduces your dependence on others—be they weak links within your organization or news media outside it. In some cases, in fact, the existence of this independent means of communicating can create pressure on commercial news media to pay more attention to you.

An organizational newsletter will probably pay for itself by keeping your membership so caught up in this inside view of the campaign and its financial requirements that their potential as contributors is multiplied. It gives you an easy way to develop the interest of others—potentially valuable recruits or important prospective fund contributors.

How widely it is distributed will determine how candidly it can be written. But don't be overly concerned about its falling into the hands of opponents, as long as it is devoted to progress rather than plans. Actually, one of the best things that can happen to you in a competitive situation is to have the opposition— tempted by such a flow of inside information—begin reacting to what you've chosen to reveal in the newsletter. For these are past events or immediate concerns; while opposition is disrupting its own plans to react to them, you can be preparing tomorrow's surprises on the basis of plans and arrangements not yet apparent in the newsletter.

Keep the mechanics simple. Ask the post office about a bulk rate mailing permit ($30 fee plus $15 per year), which allows you to print a permit form on envelopes rather than stamping them and to mail at reduced rates. Better still, print the return address and mailing permit on the back of the last sheet, address each copy there, and mail without envelopes. This saves both money and the time required to stuff and seal.

Any office supply dealer can tell you about simple stencil systems which enable you to address copies to your entire mailing list mechanically; this can save hours which will then be freed for direct campaigning purposes.

Don't eat up your budget having your newsletter printed; it's "all in the family," so no one will mind informality. Even outsiders (the press, potential recruits or contributors) who are on your list will realize from its informal nature that they're being let in on semi-private (and thus unusually candid) terms.

So stick to the mimeograph machine, the spirit duplicator, or some other inexpensive system which can be operated by volunteers and only requires a typewriter for composition. If it's mimeograph, obtain a set of styluses so that you can draw on the stencil as well as type; charts and maps and diagrams will often facilitate communication.

Be sure you've chosen a system for which equipment is readily available. If necessary, include funds in your budget to purchase or rent used equipment so that your communication machinery can be thrown into gear at any time. It will be a good investment.

The combination of chain-of-command communication, special telephoning teams, meetings as necessary, publicity through news media (and bulletin boards and other available media), and your own newsletter should enable you to "play" your organization like a piano—timing each element in the flow of information for maximum impact on your recruits, the public, and even the opposition.

The essence of leadership is management; the essence of management is control; in a volunteer organization, the essence of control is communication.

PART THREE

The showdown

Managing the Showdown

When It's Time to Close Up Shop

CHAPTER FOURTEEN

Managing the showdown

A good campaign plan will peak in the last few days before the community is called upon to make its decision. Like a boxer who has overtrained, a campaign which peaks too early will come to a dull ending—one which inspires little excitement in an already bored public and a low level of enthusiasm and energy from already tired or overconfident campaign workers.

In the planning of your campaign, you should pace your activities with this final phase in mind. Don't spring all of your research on the public at once; don't say everything you've got to say at the beginning. To keep the press, the public, and your own organization interested, you must be capable of injecting something new into the community dialogue at regular intervals throughout the project.

But the crescendo should build, near the end, toward a final flurry of activity which awakens the dead if necessary, dramatizing to the public that now is the time for decision and that a golden opportunity will be lost if that decision does not support your proposal.

Peaking to such a climax is normally associated with election campaigns. Too often, practitioners of the other approaches—the public opinion campaign, or the organization of a cooperative venture—forget that they have an even greater need for the mobilizing drama, the concentrated attention, which such a strategy can lend to their efforts. To illustrate:

You've collected a thousand petition signatures asking the Housing Authority to include in its budget funds for planning a low-cost housing project, to be presented to the public in the near future. But the authority is not legally obligated to act upon this petition; it is only a demonstration of public opinion.

The signature collection was organized and performed

139

over a period of several weeks. The authority's budget hearing will not take place until next month. If you simply forward the petition, or disperse your organization and assign several of the officers to accompany you to that eventual hearing to present it, the peak of public interest passes, and with it passes much of the pressure on the Housing Authority to accede to your wishes.

But instead, you keep interest alive by publicizing plans for a mass turnout of citizens at the Housing Authority's budget hearing. You create speculation as to whether the normal meetingplace will hold the crowd which is anticipated. Perhaps you increase the heat with a formal citizen's request to the authority chairman that the hearing be moved to a large auditorium. The press will love this, and the whole community can be drawn into the suspense of seeing if you make good on your predictions of a crowd.

Now your entire organization can be remobilized around a specific task—one which will inevitably bring public interest to a peak at exactly the right moment (the hearing at which the authority decides what to do about your petition)—because only at that moment will the suspense be resolved by the actual size of the crowd you are able to produce.

Cooperative ventures (and some public opinion campaigns) may lack any preordained moment-of-decision which can serve as an anchor for your peaking strategy. In that case, creating a deliberate countdown for the achievement of your goal can serve the same purpose. For instance:

You're attempting to raise $20,000 to buy an old, vacant, historic building and convert it into a community museum. You've made your case through publicity and prepared potentially major contributors with advance mailings. But you want to draw as much of the community as possible into the project, to give it a sustained base of future support, and you've planned a door-to-door solicitation for small contributions covering the entire town.

Your solicitors have been recruited and instructed and assigned to specific blocks. You can cover the community in one weekend (with a back-up effort the next weekend to reach people who weren't at home).

You obtain sign locations at several major traffic or shopping centers and prepare displays there which can show from hour to hour what total has been reached. You contract for hourly radio spots to further announce your totals, as an inducement to the local station to include your frequent progress reports in its news broadcasts throughout the weekend. Your canvassers are instructed to call in every hour or two, to add their results to the growing total.

Now you've couched your final phase in elements of drama and suspense which will have people anticipating those canvassers as they answer their doorbells. You've given the entire community an opportunity to get into the act, to help make the news which is unfolding before them.

The impact of such peaking tactics is not confined to the general public. They put your organization under a spotlight and exert pressure on all recruits to give their best to this final service they can render the cause.

This final phase of intense activity will be a hectic one for leaders. It must be kept brief, extending no longer than an intense level of public attention and organizational activity can be sustained. This means too little time for replanning, for complex adjustments, for replacing manpower, for extensive communication up and down the chair of command.

It is therefore essential that all plans be completed down to the last foreseeable detail well in advance of this showdown period, while calm consideration is possible, while broad perspectives still override momentary crises. The plan must be communicated to every member of the organization with thoroughness and care, because there will be little time to ask questions, to request supplementary decisions once the curtain goes up on this concluding drama.

It is important that everybody know as much as possible about the entire plan, not just specifically assigned roles, so that willing volunteers who see things breaking down around them can spring into the breech and correct such breakdowns on their own initiative, without conflicting with other aspects of the plan. (In fact, unless they understand the total context of their own functions, they may not be able to recognize breakdowns which they could easily remedy.)

It has been said that the massive invasion of Hitler's Fortress Europa by allied forces in 1944 was led not by generals, but by sergeants and second lieutenants. The generals had planned for every foreseeable eventuality, but when the troops hit the beaches, an incredible number of variables came into play—enemy reactions, the human frailty of individual commanders, the sudden looming of unexpected opportunities, etc. For a few hours, with hundreds of individual actions rendering tight control from the top impossible, the men who led small squads and platoons decided the fate of an epic undertaking, because while they may not have known what was happening over the next hill, they knew the grand design. Their individual initiatives in pushing each small segment of the invasion—right there under their noses—in the direction of that grand design constitute a chapter of history fraught with significance for leaders of the climactic phase of any enterprise.

As you go into this final phase, some deliberate talk about such individual initiative is in order. Discussion of contingencies—one last round of that "What if?" game—will keep your volunteers alert to problems and opportunities. Without such deliberate discussion, the reticent may not even realize that they have permission to improvise.

This is the last round. You can afford to burn out the energies, the commitment of your manpower, in quest of maximum performance.

It is frequently essential, in this final phase, to shatter your organization into small components. Over-all supervision will be difficult, because of time factors and the necessary focusing of attention on the work at hand rather than the chain of command.

If possible, you should eliminate all requirements for communication and coordination and supervision beyond the scope of each team of volunteers which is actually, physically working together—in immediate contact with each other—except for those progress reports which enable you to sustain the over-all drama and spot major crises or emergencies.

But don't simply point people in the right direction and leave them on their own. Maintain some driving force, some psychological pressure, which will push individual efforts toward their limits. Keep top-echelon leaders moving about the community during the climax, letting every worker know that someone is watching.

Your own inspection tours can have a decisive effect on morale. Particularly in the case of a political candidate, personal appearances on the front lines during the heat of the final push will help keep everyone working through the last productive minute. And during this climax, leaders actually have more time for such activity than earlier, because most of their work is done.

Too often, project leaders turn themselves back into foot soldiers at this stage of the game—and try to improve the results by collecting signatures or distributing handbills themselves. If you have a large number of middle-echelon supervisors who will be relatively inactive during the climax, it may be feasible to use them to augment basic manpower. But the people at the top can usually accomplish more as roving observers, as morale builders for the total organization, than they can as individual bottom-rung campaigners.

Maintain a flexible reserve of mobile manpower, including supervisory troubleshooters, for this final push. Inevitably, some things will break down. The pattern of progress reports will indicate the problem areas. There won't be time to examine what has happened and reorganize the people on the scene. Tomorrow it won't matter if a few feathers have been ruffled by duplication of effort. The quick dispatch of mobile teams to substitute for nonfunctioning or malfunctioning units of the campaign may provide the margin between failure and success.

Additional impetus toward energetic performance can be provided by announced celebration plans. Entice your volunteers to anticipate the big party that final evening—after the polls have closed or the funds have been deposited. When they're looking forward to sociably comparing notes, they'll work harder to insure that those comparisons will be personally gratifying.

Be prepared yourself—psychologically, and with substitute manpower or contingency plans—for some of your people to fall apart. A volunteer community campaign involves people in strange exercises, often contrasting sharply to the normal work situations in which experience and status have given them self-confidence. The greatest fear of many volunteers is not the failure of the enterprise, but exposure to personal failure in the eyes of a group of people who've become valued comrades. When such failures loom before them, they may lose sight of the fact that even partial performance contributes to the over-all goal and creates far less disruption in a coordinated effort than does a sudden vacuum. They may construct farfetched excuses to opt out—to remove themselves from the project and the tension before they fail, but after it's too late to replace them.

At this stage of the game, little can be gained by aggressive discipline. When you sense that you've pushed an insecure individual as far as possible, let up. Settle for a partial performance, and make the volunteer concerned feel as good about the value of that performance as possible. Throw in your floating reserves, if feasible, to repair the damage.

A final observation about the visible mental state of the person at the top: Every organization, during the climactic phase, walks a thin line between panic and overconfidence; it is your role to keep it poised exactly on that line—spurred to energetic performance by a high sense of urgency, yet dissuaded from unwise expedients or that collapse of effort which accompanies a sense of impending defeat.

We said earlier that a good meeting was a work of dramatic art and that conducting it was like directing a play. Leadership during the climax of a campaign may better be compared to a challenging acting assignment.

You're Gary Cooper, walking down that dusty street at high noon. Others realize how much is at stake—what is demanded of them—by your own obvious decision to make an extreme commitment. Yet others learn there is no need for panic because you are calm, and the gods have not struck you dead.

The first element in your act is a prediction of victory— one always accompanied by reference to the closeness of the race, to offset overconfidence. Just as we suggested in the beginning that evidence of the plausibility of a basic proposal was a necessary condition of recruiting, here in the final phase an expectation of victory is essential to the intense burst of commitment needed for the climax.

One of the hardest tasks of a leader is to display such confidence even when you don't really feel it. Nothing can bring a campaign to a halt as quickly as an admission from the person at the top—the real expert, in the eyes of the organization—that defeat is probable.

So resist the temptation to let people down easily by preparing them psychologically for possible defeat. Be prepared to make your alibis later, if they're necessary to restore your credibility as a community leader. But as you move into that final phase, predict victory openly and confidently.

The prediction will do more than encourage your troops. It will, if convincing, win you the support of hesitant citizens who have not made up their minds, but would climb on a bandwagon for the gratification of being with a winner.

And your victory prediction will provide one last occasion for free press publicity. Journalists, in their race to display how fast they get the news, have a special fascination for reporting it before it happens. Anything you have to say which seems to help them do it—to prove later that "we weren't surprised"— will fall on sympathetic ears in the newsroom. The fact that the prediction is in your name gets them off the hook if you're wrong.

It is vital in this climax phase that you be prepared to completely ignore the opposition. The mythology of local politics holds a special place for the last-minute smear. But if you've presented your case well in the weeks before the showdown, you can do little more in replying to a smear than repeat what you've already said.

And attempting to reply has two serious disadvantages.

First, it publicizes the smear to people who may not even have been aware of it; getting wide distribution of any charge in the hectic climax of a campaign is a difficult task; don't help your opponent accomplish it.

Secondly, diverting attention and time and resources to respond to a smear can disrupt your planned operation, which should have been designed to make maximum use of all available manpower and resources. The most successful smears are those which cause you to interrupt your own plan and dance to the opposition's tune.

If you're opposed by people you suspect are capable of unfair tactics during the showdown, the best way to deal with them is to alert the public to the possibility; the last-minute smear is such standard mythology that the average citizen is fully capable of recognizing it. But don't create sympathy for the opposition by charging it with unethical potentiality which has not yet been demonstrated. Simply incorporate into your final publicity releases a human interest quote from your admonition to your own organization not to be panicked by such last-minute surprises. Then you haven't said one will occur, you've simply reminded everybody of the possibility.

And so, the climax draws to a conclusion. You reach that empty moment when there is nothing more to be done. On to the celebration party!

The author would not dream of spoiling your fun by attempting to describe techniques for throwing a celebration party.

CHAPTER FIFTEEN

When it's time to close up shop

When you're finished—quit.

That is perhaps one of the least recognized principles of volunteer organizations. Once all that human machinery has been assembled and lubricated, and has enjoyed the experience of flexing its muscles, people hate to dismantle it.

The civic landscape is cluttered with the pointless skeletons of organizations which have long since served their purpose, but have refused to go out of business. Often the new purposes they adopt as an excuse to continue functioning are far removed from their original objectives.

"No harm done," you might say. "Why shouldn't they keep going as long as anyone is willing to man the helm? At least it's a good excuse for good people to associate."

Effective community activists are not in over-supply. The major impediment to recruitment is the number of obligations effective people already have—many of them to barely functioning residues of no longer relevant ventures.

After you've set up one organization, you know the people and the techniques and the community factors which will enable you to repeat the process in a minimum of time. Let go; give other good causes a chance; give the claims you're making on your volunteers a vacation—so you'll be in good standing for later claims.

Remember that even a successful campaign has taught you a great deal about basic plans and arrangements which could be improved the next time around. A successful political candidate who is willing to dismantle the campaign organization is thus freer to pick a new campaign manager the next time around—or try a different basic approach. A successful public opinion campaign may lead to accusations of a "special interest group" or

147

"suspicious clique" if its organization remains in existence for the next available issue.

And if you've lost, it makes even more sense to dismantle—to start all over again without the encumbrance of basic arrangements which contributed to your defeat.

A few formalities will be necessary after the public decision. You may have to file public reports of campaign financing; you'll want to thank those who helped you; if you expect to try again, prove you're a nice guy by congratulating those who beat you, or consoling those you beat.

But above all, sift your records for the reusable residue. Those lists of leaders of various segments of the community, that carefully prepared background research, your press contacts, your identification of potential fund contributors (no longer speculative, since you've now gotten money from the best ones), those time-consuming maps on which you've divided the community into feasible door-to-door canvassing assignments, those phone numbers which tell you where to get inexpensive printing —and most particularly, the complete list of people who were willing to work, with their phone numbers for fast future contact —are valuable resources. Preserve them—and share them with other interested members of the organization. The next great idea for community innovation may be theirs.

It is this residue of people who have worked together, who know each other's interests and capabilities, which creates the most lasting effect of any community improvement project. They become a civic militia, potentially ready to spring back into action whenever local government fails to come to grips with problems or to seize upon obvious opportunities.

The existence of such an informal militia, once its effectiveness has been demonstrated by your project, will have a healthy effect on local government. Now the people running that government know that someone is looking over their shoulders.

Creating this atmosphere may do more to improve your community than the actual accomplishment of your specific project goal.

The necessity for putting something down on paper, in organized and understandable form, is perhaps the best planning discipline operating on the leaders of voluntary enterprises.

The six documents in the appendices demonstrate the point. They are sample documents in the career of a hypothetical community improvement venture: the chairman's agenda outline for the organizational meeting, a news release announcing the results of that meeting, and the four basic documents discussed in Chapter Seven—the timetable, organization chart, budget, and by-laws.

In examining these samples, note how thoroughly it was necessary to plan the CSC campaign before these documents could be put into written form. Requiring such written documents is a sound means of insuring thorough planning.

APPENDIX I: *Sample agenda notes for organizational meeting*

Organizational Meeting, Counseling Services Cooperative Centerville High School Auditorium, 8:00 P.M., September 23

8:00—Call to order, introduce self as spokesman for group of interested citizens who have been investigating community mental health problems and facilities, remind audience that it has right of private citizens to take collective action. *No action required.*

8:03—Invite nominations for temporary chairman; yield chair to Carl Hager if another nomination is made from floor. *Vote required.*

8:08—Invite nominations for temporary clerk. *Vote required.*

8:10—Outline of feasible courses of action—Hager. Motion to form CSC—Hager. Motion to delay action until citizens research group has reported—Carter. *Vote required.*

8:15—Background report on community counseling needs— Carter. *No action required.*

8:25—Background report on existing community costs from mental problems—Haynes. *No action required.*

8:30—Background report on probable costs of a public or cooperative service—Randolph. *No action required.*

8:35—Reintroduction of motion to organize—Hager. (Wording should coincide with Article I of proposed by-laws.) Invite discussion. *Vote required.*

8:45—Report of informal by-law committee—Sullivan. Motion

to adopt proposed by-laws. Invite discussion. *Vote required.*

8:55—Invite nominations for president; yield chair to temporary clerk if another nomination is made from floor. *Vote required.*

9:00—Invite nominations for vice president. *Vote required.*

9:05—Invite nominations for secretary. *Vote required.*

9:09—Invite nominations for treasurer. *Vote required.*

9:13—Invite nominations for three directors-at-large. *Vote required.*

9:20—Outline proposed initial course of action—Jones. Motion by Hager to endorse said outline as sense of meeting. *Vote required.*

9:30—Call Executive Board meeting for 8:00 P.M. next Tuesday, 15 Maplewood Drive. *No action required.*

9:33—Ask all participants to sign roster before they leave, if they are willing to work. Invite them to pay dues to Kirsch before they leave. Inform them first assignments will be phoned after Executive Board meeting. *No action required.*

9:34—Invite discussion of next need for general meeting. Motion by Hager to hold it same time and place November 4, for fund drive report. *Vote required.*

9:40—Invite motion to adjourn. *Vote required.*

9:45—Informal arrangements for news release; delegate secretary and Hager.

APPENDIX II: *Sample publicity release*

* *NEWS: For release September 24*

** For more information contact:
John Jones, President
Counseling Services Cooperative
Phone 993-4207

*** CITIZENS FORM SELF-FINANCED COOPERATIVE
TO PROVIDE FAMILY, YOUTH,
PSYCHIATRIC COUNSELING

* Centerville, September 24—Forty-seven Centerville residents converted a public discussion of mental health problems at the High School Auditorium last night into the formation of a new community service to provide professional counseling for troubled families, adults and young people.

Prompt action was facilitated by the group's decision to finance the new Counseling Services Cooperative from private contributions, plus modest fees from those who can afford them. Since no public funds are requested, the only official sanction which the group will request is a city license to offer professional services to the public, under the terms of existing state safeguards.

John Jones, 15 Maplewood Drive, was elected president of the new organization. Mrs. Arthur Marx is vice president. Miss Charlene Darby was named secretary, and Dr. Alexander Kirsch will serve as treasurer.

Jones announced the appointment of Carl Hager to head an initial fund-raising drive, and James Carter to investigate the availability of qualified part-time professional counselors.

Carter, whose report of preliminary investigations by a group of citizen volunteers prompted the decision to organize CSC, pointed out that 9 per cent of Centerville's high school students were involved in incidents requiring police action last year. He quoted psychiatric evidence that teen-age delinquency was often related to family problems or parental instability.

"It will take $20,000 to open an office and provide services for a six-month trial period," Hager told the group. "For most of us, a $100 annual contribution is cheap insurance against domestic tragedies—and a good investment in the community. Every dollar we raise and spend will save the city several dollars in court and police costs. Our task now is to find at least 200 families who agree that this is a bargain they—as good citizens, don't want to pass up."

**** Hager said he would announce specific plans for the fund drive after an Executive Board meeting next Tuesday evening.

** encl: CSC By-Laws adopted by September 23 meeting

---

* Release date assures all media they've gotten equal treatment.

** Verification contact and by-law enclosure assure media the report is valid and authoritative.

*** Headline is your brief opportunity to convince a busy editor that this particular release is worth his attention; he gets dozens daily.

**** Always leave yourself an obvious opening for a subsequent release if possible.

APPENDIX III: *Sample project timetable*

CALENDAR: *Counseling Services Cooperative Fund Drive*

PRELIMINARY

	EXEC. COMM.	CANVASS	PUBLICITY	SPECIAL TEAMS
Sept. 7	Meet Mayor			
8			Mayor story with photos	
15			Announce organizational meeting	
16–22				Meeting attendance build-up

PHASE I

	EXEC. COMM.	CANVASS	PUBLICITY	SPECIAL TEAMS
Sept. 23	Organizational meeting			
24			Report organization	
25–29	Get license			
26–2			Recruit survey teams	
30	Plans meeting			
Oct. 1			Report survey, licensing, dinner plans	
1–14				Professional interviews
3–5		Interest survey		

PHASE II

	EXEC. COMM.	CANVASS	PUBLICITY	SPECIAL TEAMS
Oct. 4–18				Dinner arrangements
6–18		Dinner ticket sales		
8			Report survey results, plug dinner	
14	Meet professionals			
15			Story on professionals as dinner guests	
18				Dinner
18–23		Recruit solicitors		Countdown letters to special prospects
(Showdown Oct. 23–26)				
23		Solicitor meeting		
24–26		CANVASS WEEKEND!		

PHASE III

	EXEC. COMM.	CANVASS	PUBLICITY	SPECIAL TEAMS
Oct. 26	Canvass report party			
29			Report canvass results	
31–2			Catch-up weekend	
Nov. 3	Rent office			
4	General membership Report meeting			
5			Announce opening	

APPENDIX IV: *Sample organization chart*

ORGANIZATION: *Counseling Services Cooperative Fund Drive*

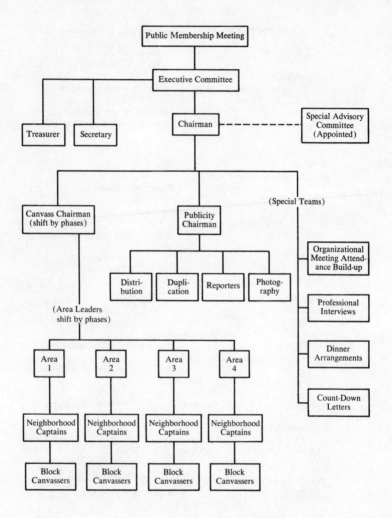

APPENDIX V: *Sample project budget*

BUDGET: *Counseling Services Cooperative Fund Drive*

DATE	ITEM	INCOME	COST	BALANCE
23 Sept.	Dues from Organizational Meeting	$ 50.00		$ 50.00
23 Sept.	Auditorium Rental		$ 10.00	40.00
25 Sept.	Licensing Fee		5.00	35.00
30 Sept.	Dues from Recruiting	50.00		85.00
1 Oct.	Printing Questionnaires		30.00	55.00
5 Oct.	Dues Collected During Survey	30.00		85.00
5 Oct.	Printing Tickets for Dinner		15.00	70.00
* 10 Oct.	Advance Dinner Tickets (Exec. Comm.)	35.00		105.00
10 Oct.	Deposit to Dinner Caterer		100.00	5.00
18 Oct.	Dinner Ticket Sales (200 each $5)	1000.00		1005.00
18 Oct.	Banquet Hall Rental		50.00	955.00
18 Oct.	Caterer (207 dinners, $4 each, less deposit)		728.00	227.00
18 Oct.	Brochures, Letterheads, Envelopes		60.00	167.00
19 Oct.	Postage for Countdown Letters		35.00	132.00
19 Oct.	Mimeographing Letters		10.00	122.00
** RESERVE FOR CONTINGENCIES, ETC.				$122.00

---

* Note necessity for special arrangements (advance ticket payment by officers) to meet anticipated point of insufficient funds (deposit to caterer). Advance budgeting reveals such crises while there's time to plan countermoves.

** The major contingency possibility is, of course, not unexpected expenses, but unexpectedly low ticket sales. This budget allows for possible 12 per cent difference in goal and actual sales.

APPENDIX VI: *Sample by-laws*

BY-LAWS: *Counseling Services Cooperative*

Article I—Establishment of Cooperative

Section 1—The purposes of this organization shall be to establish, raise funds for, and oversee operations of a nonprofit agency available to the general public of the Town of Centerville for family, youth, and psychiatric counseling by qualified professionals.

Section 2—The Name of this organization shall be "Counseling Services Cooperative of Centerville."

Article II—Membership

Section 1—Full ultimate authority for the direction of Counseling Services Cooperative shall be vested in its general membership meetings, at which every member in good standing is entitled to participate and vote.

Section 2—Any legal resident of Centerville who pays an annual membership fee of $5, due each September 1, shall be considered a member in good standing.

Article III—Officers

The officers of Counseling Services Cooperative shall include a President, a Vice President, a Secretary, a Treasurer, and three Directors-at-Large; said seven officers shall together constitute the Executive Committee.

Section 1—It shall be the duty of the President to preside over all general membership and Executive Committee meetings,

158

to represent the organization on public occasions, and to make such appointments from the general membership as he shall deem advisable for the effective conduct of the work of the organization.

Section 2—It shall be the duty of the Vice President to assist the President as the latter requests, to represent the organization on appropriate public occasions, and to preside over the Special Advisory Committee.

Section 3—It shall be the duty of the Secretary to record the proceedings of all general membership and Executive Committee meetings, to maintain adequate records of the organization's activities, and to conduct such official correspondence as shall be required.

Section 4—It shall be the duty of the Treasurer to collect, safeguard, disburse, and make periodic reports of all funds obtained in the name of the organization. The Treasurer shall maintain separate accounts of funds obtained for the preliminary fund-raising program and those obtained for subsequent operation of the Cooperative.

Section 5—It shall be the duty of the Executive Committee to act in behalf of the general membership between meetings of said body.

Article IV—Special Advisory Committee

The President, with approval of the Executive Committee, shall be entitled to appoint individuals from the general membership—or from the community at large, regardless of membership—to a Special Advisory Committee; the function of this committee shall be to advise the Executive Board on matters requiring special insights or a broad range of perspectives; the recommendations of this committee shall be purely advisory, and shall not be binding upon the Executive Committee.

Article V—Accountability for Funds

Section 1—No expenditure of funds shall be authorized except on approval of five members of the Executive Committee, or a majority vote of a general membership meeting.

Section 2—A complete report of receipts and disbursements shall be deposited monthly by the Treasurer at the Public Library or at the Town Clerk's office, for inspection by the interested public.

Article VI—Membership Meetings

Section 1—The general membership shall conduct an annual meeting and election of officers the first Tuesday of each September, at a time and place to be announced at least two weeks in advance by the Executive Committee.

Section 2—Additional general membership meetings shall be called by the Executive Committee when it deems such meetings necessary, or when presented with a request for such a meeting signed by ten members of the organization, provided one-week advance notice is given the general membership before any such meeting.

Article V—Amendment

These By-laws may be amended by a majority vote of any general membership meeting.